UNITED NATIONS
UNLOCKED

UNITED NATIONS UNLOCKED

The Missing Link the UN Needs to Tackle Global Terrorism and the Coming Tech Tsunami

By

Karen Judd Smith

www.StrategicSolutions.onl

GDG
PRESS

ISBN: 978-0-692-81235-8

Acknowledgements

Each of us stands upon the shoulders of our ancestors
and the society of which they were part. We draw upon their
wisdom, knowledge and insight often without realizing it.

With all that to stand on, I now have front row seats for a
new explosion—of remarkable technologies that change the
way we extend ourselves into, and interact with, one another
and the world.

This book would not have taken shape without the
ancients, my contemporaries and technology alike, inspiring,
challenging, and shaping my world.

Contrary to my own plans for a life in the sciences, I
ended up spending more than 20 years working with people
who sought to make our world better—through politics,
activism, religion and service to humanity in and through
the work of the United Nations. In the midst of all this, I was
honored to meet and at times work with some of the most
noble and brave souls, many putting a good part or even all
of their lives on the line.

For those who still labor daily to make our world a better place, thank you, for all you do.

Then there are those who helped me here in the Bay Area in a more hands-on way: with their encouragement, feedback, daily support, edits, and ideas.

It cannot be easy to live with a non-writer, caged in by her efforts to put ideas onto paper, desperate to slow the tide of thoughts into a trickle so that they could be transmuted into some 36,000 words all laid out in one long line—all of which are meant to make sense!

Therefore, to Kevin, my husband of more than 30 years, and my longtime colleague and friend, Marilyn Morris, who not only collaborated, but also, and more importantly, stayed with me through these six months of this book writing process, thank you.

Contents

INTRODUCTION
A Crucial Pivot Point

Pivot points of strategic change have always caught my attention. The importance of these was first driven home while growing up on our farm in the Riverina, in southern New South Wales, Australia. There were always bags or bales, equipment or animals to move from one place to another, and often I didn't have sufficient muscle, reach or tools within proximity. As is the norm on farms, I had to improvise. In the process, I discovered what it meant to create leverage, produce torque and consider the mindset of the other—especially animals—even when needing to perform seemingly simple tasks.

Reason did not seem to work that well on our fearful young calves, nor the incorrigible massive bristly boars, let alone the antsy and amply-horned bulls! Muscles were helpful, but teamwork and innovation were often essential to get us through those days of harvesting crops, herding cattle, sheep, chickens and pigs, loading and unloading bags of grain, fertilizer, potatoes or bales of hay, often while temperatures hung for hours over 110 degrees in the shade.

In almost everything we did, we had opportunities to devise and improve how we would get things done. We learned from a young age, how success and failure in each task often turned on a dime, and in a split second.

Later, as a physics major with a minor in history and philosophy of science at the University of Melbourne, I began to notice other kinds of pivot points and how they shaped history. These were ideas, paradigms, and inventions. Each of these revolutionized human affairs, moving whole cultures and societies into new territory and directions of action.

Another important piece that accompanies pivot points and which has impacted my focus over the years came from a simple piece of advice I was given one day by a mentor of sorts, Peter Fong.

Peter had escaped a Communist POW camp with his co-pilot and lifelong friend in the 1950s. By the time I met him in Jakarta while traveling as a backpacking student in the mid-1970's (as many an Aussie did in those days), he had built a strong international trading business out of Singapore. One day while playing squash there he urged me to, "Anticipate. Keep your eye on what is coming and be ready for it." That one exhortation to anticipate has been with me ever since.

Throughout my extraordinarily varied adult life, I have continued to look for pivotal moments and have sought to understand what triggers them. The 3D framework for change leadership outlined in this book encompasses the ideological artifacts of my lifelong interest and inquiry into this topic.

What fascinates me is that whatever old thought or pattern of behavior that leads up to these critical moments can be changed, and sometimes in one fell swoop. We then see things differently after that, and the impact of this is lasting. Call it a paradigm change, a Gestalt shift that takes place intellectually, emotionally or spiritually, a change of mind or an aha moment, the way we see the world, and our relationship with it, is never the same again.

Many people today recognize that humanity as a whole is approaching a pivot point that will have a proportionally larger impact on us than anything we have experienced before. There are substantive reasons to make such claims. The technology revolution is impacting everything: our social lives, our work, and our political and economic systems. It is increasingly a dominant factor in human affairs.

Some go so far as to give this pivot point a date and a name that carries with it the weighty equivalence of the cosmological beginnings: singularity. Futurist Ray Kurzweil, for example, likes the date of 2029 as the time when human life will be irreversibly transformed to where we transcend the biological limitation of our bodies and brains. Philosopher Nick Bostrom meanwhile outlines the possible explosion of artificial intelligence (AI) into superintelligence in the coming decades and explores the resultant, multitudinous consequences.

While these are fascinating discussions, this book is focused more on what it is we can do to re-balance the currently growing and increasingly problematic bifurcation of our technological and social dimensions. I maintain that so much of today's socio-political turbulence that we experience such as terrorism, financial upheaval, food shortages and climate crises are less about what many see as an impending tech tsunami, along with energy and other resource issues, and more about our lagging social structures that resist innovation.

Instead of running parallel with our technological advancements, our social institutions are not keeping up with the decentralization processes that are underway, spearheaded by today's technologies. It is this difference that is creating unnecessary shearing forces and tensions in the human social fabric.

While we are busy ogling the latest technologies (and like you, I love the latest technologies), we forget to adjust for the impact it will have on our lives. At the personal level, we sometimes long for what was, going through a short period of denial, anger, bargaining and finally acceptance. We eventually make the accompanying changes and begin to fall in love with the new norm. Our social institutions are far less amenable and frankly, were not built to facilitate change.

It is upon this critical missing piece that I wish to focus, for like it or not, we are social animals and it is within our social systems that technology is incubated and innovated. Therefore, it is also critical that our social institutions and mechanisms—and the UN in particular—are also able to upgrade so as to appropriately respond to the ubiquitous impact of technology upon these institutions as well as our personal lives.

As an active participant in the civil society of the United Nations for the last twenty years, I have been watching and waiting for the UN to grasp the great and terrible wonder of technology and its global impact, and to seriously consider in a more proactive way, the implications for the UN and the world it intends to safeguard. What I see—actually what I don't see—is becoming increasingly distressful with every swing of the pendulum in the United Nations Headquarters lobby.

The gap between the UN and the tech world is growing and this does not bode well for the future of the UN, and therefore for humanity. The UN has very little institutional interest in technology. Meanwhile, those in the tech world, if their attention is drawn to it, might be fascinated by the idea of the UN for about ten seconds, and then they would go straight back to their real issues and interests in fields such as predictive and prescriptive analytics, coding and tech start-ups.

However, both parties have something the other urgently needs. The UN has a mountaintop view and access to the political world through social relationships and political mechanisms. Tech entrepreneurs use mathematic and scientific principles as their tools, while their views are shaped through the iterative scramble for innovation and new technologies. The tech world largely dwells in the midst of a kind of tech primordial soup focused on what is coming. The UN seeks to extend its 20th century system of governance and deployment in hopes that it can yet manage the shifting and changing political waters of the 21st-century.

Neither side is particularly aware of, or interested enough in, the other to forge a partnership of any kind. However, I believe that meaningful engagement between the two is most urgent. The gap between these two is perhaps the most innovative space we could hope to tap into today. The potential of the dynamic interplay of these two currently divergent worlds could impact us all in a very positive way.

If this is indeed the case, the question then becomes, not if, but how soon can these two widely different groups with dramatically different world-views begin to engage one another? How can the UN accommodate the agile, nimble, quick-to-start-up and move-on mindset that drives the tech world? How can those energetic and often brilliant techies be inspired to look up from their ingenious devices and see the bigger picture, the whole of humanity scope in which the UN goes about its daily work and even more, feel compelled to assist the UN in its daunting task?

How the UN and the tech world can be drawn together into meaningful engagement is what this book endeavors to demonstrate. I will make the case that these two communities need to work together on issues in common. I will also describe exactly what kind of innovative leadership is required for such a partnership to be forged.

Further, I will show how the UN can employ a strategy within its august environment that will open it to the new kind of thinking and way of doing that is widely embraced in the tech community. Lastly, I will briefly suggest several steps, all quite doable, that the UN can take to ensure that its partnership with the tech community generates vital discussions and actions toward making the world much safer.

There are a few concepts in this book that are not only useful for the UN and tech community, but also invaluable to individuals in their personal endeavors. My intent is for these concepts to be used in a specific way at the UN, but if they are also personally helpful, please feel free to use them. Much of that material is in the appendix and I indicate where it is in applicable areas of the book.

I will be discussing some concepts of leadership not commonly held or widely used, especially in larger, established entities such as the UN. In that regard, let me address the key words and concepts involved up front so they will feel more familiar to you when you encounter them again in later chapters.

The word that best conveys innovative leadership to distinguish it from the more traditional management leadership is "transilience." It means having the ability and capacity to leap across gaps or divides. Transilience is the kind of leadership that today's constantly changing world needs.

How to acquire the mindset for this kind of leadership requires awareness of its elements. This is addressed in the section where I explain a "3D model of leadership." There are also personal skills one can readily utilize to become more adept at leading in a transilient way. A tool that builds these life-navigation skills is described in Appendix A where I outline the "5 Questions of the Solutions Matrix™."

If you resonate with the premise that small changes accumulate to effect bigger changes, and that strategic changes combine to make a difference that is a tangible difference (i.e., it actually works), this book will have some intriguing new things for you to think about.

If you also have wanted to see the UN become more relevant in a world where things now change at the speed of light, and have admired the spirit and energy of the tech community that pushes the edge of that lightning pace, this book should inspire you. I believe there is hope that the two can indeed become partners.

However, the overall intent of this book is a bit wider in scope than just the bonus of intriguing and inspiring readers. The world sorely needs the UN to step up and match the agility and innovation, if from behind the scenes, that the tech community would bring as a core strength were it to enter into such a partnership.

The tech community likewise needs to acknowledge its exponentially increasing impact on world affairs, and engage the UN as to how it can make those impacts in a humanity-friendly and -enhancing, not -endangering, manner.

All this in a nutshell proposes that a new partnership between the United Nations and leaders of technology be forged, so that they create a pivot point from which a new trajectory for humanity is made more secure and importantly, greater than what it was before. We simply can't be looking backward to the way we were—smaller, more isolated—as our ideal for tomorrow's greatness.

This new direction requires significant degrees of mindfulness of the need for a place in our thinking for all humanity, if we are to promote social progress and better standards of life in larger freedom.[1]

This partnership I believe will be a difference that makes a *real* difference, and one that we, all the people on planet earth urgently need, if we are going to go into the future with any significant hope of it being a brighter and better place.

Thus, to the dreamers and those transilient leaders who dare to do more than dream ...

PART I
A Window of Opportunity

CHAPTER ONE
A Tech Tsunami
& A Global Village

This book is for pragmatic visionaries, the kind who take on big issues while holding their own feet to the fires of "Is it doable? Will it work? Will it make a significant difference?" What's more, they dare, uninvited, because they are leaders.

In our increasingly tech-driven world, we are not only dealing with new technologies unthinkable just a few years ago, but we do so today at an unprecedented rate. No one has to look beyond his or her mobile device(s) to know how fast the changes are and the impact they are having on our lives. Our computers update themselves overnight while the self-driving cars of tomorrow are being road tested today.

The myriad of these and other changes are taking us into new social and political territories. Here, however, not everything is keeping pace. There is a growing gap between our rate of adoption of physically based electronic, material and biotechnologies and the rate of adaptation in our social and political systems.

Why is this important? Technological development and human life don't happen in a vacuum. In fact, without the proper social, economic and political circumstances, these innovations wouldn't be taking place today. Why would it then be any less important for the social systems and institutions that enabled this technological boom to continue to adapt and change?

Many corporate entities that didn't adapt organizationally to the external social and economic environment have died out or have begun fading. Just ask Borders Books, Lehman Brothers, Xerox, Blockbuster, Blackberry, Polaroid, MySpace and Yahoo. Today, cornerstone stores such as Macy's and The Gap are struggling with declining customer traffic, the very things that once made them large and vigorous. Human patterns of behavior are changing and our social organizations and institutions—business, social, political and educational—are also being asked to change. However, knowing or even feeling a need doesn't mean those in charge understand how to go about making the right changes in time, before their demise sets in.

Strategic agility is what is needed to remain relevant and capable of functioning effectively. This is no less true for the United Nations, our established world level body that is arguably needed more today than it was post-WWII. Today's more powerful threats appear more frequently with growing domains of impact.

You could say that technology is throwing down a gauntlet to our social and political endeavors. With every tech improvement; with every increase in speed; every increase of data analyzed and turned into information, knowledge, and insight; with every new connection made using machine learning and artificial intelligence, there is a shortened time-to-impact.

This increasing speed challenges our capacity to adapt psychologically, socially and politically as individuals and as a society. If this gap becomes perilously wide, beyond the tensile strength of our institutions, we may find ourselves in even more grave danger-zones.

If we innovated and upgraded our social organizations at the same rate as we do our technologies, there would be fewer problems. There would be fewer shearing forces between the two to add to our woes. But this difference will continue to cause the tsunami-like upheaval with growing impact in every sector of society.

As noted, technological innovations in and of themselves are not necessarily problematic. Of course, there are exceptions, with the more worrisome being the militarization of technologies, and the ever-present potential for misappropriation and misuse of technologies by those with criminal or terrorist intent.

When these challenges are then multiplied because our social capacity to integrate innovations safely into our lives and social systems also don't keep pace with technological developments, our systems and people become overwhelmed. The surge forward of by technology presses hard against the limited, slow-moving, non-adaptive social institutions. They become opposing forces. The tension between these two are akin to the tensions and stresses between the shifting tectonic plates that cause earthquakes and tsunamis. While natural, these effects can be deadly.

This book presents not only the concept of game-changing ideas for reducing those tensions between technology's surge and society's faltering structures, but also presents a specific way forward based on proven practices in both personal and organizational realms. Further, these concepts and practices are tailored for application to one organization crucial to our collective future: the United Nations (UN).

While I have written this book with two main groups in mind, the UN, and the tech community, the core points about change leadership are relevant throughout organized humanity. These two communities admittedly are not typical partners in the work of peace and security. Nonetheless, they are both already engaged in this work, albeit in their very different ways and scopes of influence.

Whether they currently see one another as partners, their futures are inextricably linked. The United Nations works in the public sector to "save succeeding generations from the scourge of war" as a family of organizations desperate to catch up with transnational criminal and terrorist elements, not to mention broiling civil wars and strained international relationships.

In the private sector, the tech community is meanwhile generating an unprecedented economic boom fueled both by the hope of economic success and visible impact on society. Technology does not automatically improve, (not yet, though there are signs on the horizon). The current surge is driven by human effort and passion that interweaves creative investment, personal striving, small, iterative successes and the endeavor to break new and meaningful scientific, technical and enterprise boundaries.

United Nations Unlocked outlines how these two groups can bring their divergent specialties and worlds of influence together in a specific, practical and potentially powerful synthesis. The difference between these two groups and the current void between them is a problem that nevertheless provides an enormous source of creative potential. What if a workable connection can be made?

No matter how implausible it may seem to many individuals within either community, it excites me to think of what will emerge from a well-structured engagement between the UN and the tech world.

Most people who are daily involved in the tech world, my three adult children for example, see little if any connection between their scientific pursuits of growing stem cells or developing apps or optimizing systems, and the UN. The latter is, after all, a world replete with arcane endeavors that take place largely behind closed doors in the General Assembly (GA), the Security Council (SC) or the Economic and Social Council (ECOSOC) over months and years with little to show for all those hours of negotiations—except more words and resolutions.

Interestingly, it is the individuals in today's tech companies developing codes, protocol and practices and those directing their work, who are becoming the architects of tomorrow's peace and security. It is in their digital world that the larger "we" is already engaged in today's warfare—cyberwars. It is in their realms that the larger "we" are already engaged in today's warfare—cyberwars.

Cyberattackers and hackers are no longer hidden in mom's basement. They form cells of their own as cybercriminals and cyberterrorists. They are being wooed and gainfully employed by governments the world over. They are busy 24/7 devising, coding and deploying Remote Access Trojans (RATs) and other malicious software that allows cybercriminals access to sensitive applications and information, including but not limited to data, passwords, and the ability to infect other sites and resources. AI attack teams capture and sabotage intelligence organizations and even reach beyond the digital realms to wreak physical destruction.

Cyber-physical strikes such as that of the Stuxnet virus are not new. In this 2010 software invasion, a computer worm grabbed the headlines when it sabotaged the centrifuge controls at the Natanz plant in Iran. This attack, in tech years, might as well have occurred eons ago. What capacity to do further damage now exists?

The emergence of the nuclear age in the last century placed all of us in a precarious position. However, nuclear proliferation is now just one strand in a growing array of emerging technologies easily turned into golems for which our society is unprepared.

It is actually very difficult to erect a nuclear plant with military capacity without detection. It is extremely expensive and takes years to bring the facility up to that level. In the meantime, other nations catch on and pressures, such as financial and other sanctions, can be brought to bear to slow or otherwise impede the militarization of such plants.

Today, hacking into an international system, be it banking, health care, defense, electrical grids and so forth, while also difficult, is readily possible and does not take decades to actuate. If you were a rogue nation wanting to create havoc in a relatively inexpensive manner and hidden from view, which would you choose?

I make no apologies for referring to earthquakes, tsunamis and nightmarish hacking scenarios with regard to technology's growing impact. I fully intend to poke your amygdala, to tap its connection with our pre-verbal responses and emotional memories, because only appealing to the rational part of your brain won't motivate you to do anything different. Don't our politicians and marketers know that well enough about us? Why do so many elections deteriorate into base scare-tactics that reduce many of us to vote according to that which we most don't want to lose?

While taking on some of the most challenging issues we face today, this book is not an effort to promote a conversation that remains in the flight or fight mode. I want to quickly get from the "What's going on?" where most of us are anxious and concerned, to "What can we do about it?" While there truly is such a thing as too little, too late, and windows of opportunity do open, *and* they also close, I believe that we still have time to shift our focus forward toward solutions, ones which can be novel, even truly great and inspiring.

Today, with the stakes leveraged by technology's prevalence in our lives, urgency is our friend. A sense of urgency is what we need to get us started to make the differences that count. As much as we all like to feel as though we had no choice when faced with making hard decisions, by acting before that time, we can avoid ending up in the red, in the crisis zone where options decrease and outcomes are far, far from ideal.

Consider for a moment that the world is but one interconnected village. What would you do, if it—we—were facing grave danger and you were given the chance to save it? Here's one quintessential story from Japan that illustrates the sense of urgency that I believe we need to feel now:

"All the villagers in a small coastal Japanese village were so busy with their preparations for a festival that only an old man high on the side of the coastal hills could see the huge tidal wave speeding toward them on the horizon. Unable to get down to the village to warn the revelers, he set fire to the rice fields they were dependent upon. At once, the villagers saw the fire and they came running to the hill to save their crops and indeed, it was they who were saved, even as their village was washed into the sea below."

The hero of the story above was rather unlikely, an old farmer. Nonetheless, first, he could see what was coming on the horizon, and second, he was able to devise a plan that worked. The third capacity he possessed, and this is critical, was the willingness to act.

We need to be like that old man, with our eyes on the horizon, our minds on solving the building wave of issues it presents, and our hearts willing to do what is required to prevent our fellow villagers from being washed out to sea.

CHAPTER TWO
Three Interlinked
Game-Changing Ideas

Let me first clarify a key point about the looming tech tsunami that is crucial to understand before we delve into three interlinked game changing ideas that are invaluable components of what this book proposes: the causes of impending turmoil are not due solely to the exponential pace of technological development. Like any tsunami, the speed of the wave becomes threatening as the water shallows and meets something immovable. The tech tsunami appears threatening because of the ill-matched rate of change of two technologies—our physical and our social technologies, the latter being seemingly relatively immovable.

Any durable solution to the growing turbulence surrounding technology's impact will not come from technology per se, but from making our social technologies—our organizations and institutions—more agile, responsive and flexible. The tech community is doing what society is rewarding it to do—evolve better and better technologies. As to any rewards for efforts to adapt and update our social technologies, survival may need to suffice for a start.

More importantly, since time is of the essence, the most expedient route will be to start with a shift in our thinking about our social institutions. In the last few years, we have seen the evolution of the telephone from being cabled and landlocked into today's mobile devices. It's time for our organizations to evolve similarly. While their charters were once upon a time written in stone, today those organizations need to evolve into agile social devices with plug and play apps appropriate to the tasks at hand.

Once untethered, the mobile phone became something unexpectedly remarkable. I maintain that the tethers of our social institutions today are old habits speaking and that it is time to build on our existing social structures in new ways. The fix may well be easier than we could ever have imagined, and especially so for the United Nations.

Of course, some will say we should slow technology down, restrict it, or make it more difficult to evolve. Not only is that unreasonable, it just won't happen. The cat is out of the bag, or more aptly, a multitude of cats are out of a myriad of bags and have scattered in every direction. No amount of herding will ever get them back in again.

Realistically, there is no way to slow the technology surge itself. The tsunami will arrive at the shore of our social institutions. The question is, what shall we do?

If we wait too long, options disappear and we are left with only drastic choices. We are left with setting the fields on fire. I propose that we not wait, and that we innovate at the UN in a way that opens room for the tech community to send its best and brightest to engage with equally interested parties concerned with the future of humanity.

What we can do is turn our attention to organizational innovation at the UN. It may seem harsh, but the UN could do with a little updating. Okay, perhaps it could do with a lot of updating. But at this juncture, I want to limit our focus in this discussion on what it needs to do with regard to technology's global impact.

There has been talk of UN renewal for years. To be quite frank, although the UN is a well-respected institution, it is also a rather outdated 20th century system. True, it is doing its best, most days heroically, to keep up with the constantly morphing threats and challenges in a globalizing, and now tech-driven world.

However, keeping up simply is not good enough to lead at the global level. Who or what will fill this growing global-level leadership vacuum? This is the core question.

The window of opportunity will not stay open forever. In any type of vacuum, someone or something will step in. For now, the UN remains the optimal convener to engage the tech community in developing a 21st century leadership change. There is no guarantee it will remain as such. Its window of opportunity is closing.

Let me get right to the point and state what I believe needs to be done. It will be my task throughout the rest of the book to appropriately unpack what this will take and to explain the terms used in the sentence below.

In response to global level challenges brought about by technology's pervasive advancements, the UN should:

Create security "meta-nets" to work in concert with the Security Council to create big opportunity, humanity level strategic initiatives in response to the peace and security issues resulting from cybersecurity and cyber-physical threats.

This statement will raise a number of questions: "What is a meta-net?" "Why involve the Security Council?" "What on earth is meant by big opportunity?" "Why begin with the issue of cybersecurity and cyber-physical threats?"

I answer these questions and more in the sections that follow, but first, I want address *the* question that many a representative to the UN or UN staffer will be asking: Does this proposal have anything to do with UN charter change?

Organizational Adaptation Not Charter Change

This is usually the game-stopper associated with any talk of significant change or renewal at the UN. I will then explain why this proposal completely avoids this problem.

The premise here is that innovation is better than irrelevance and death, and frankly, easier to do (using meta-nets) than most people would dare to think. Since the very early years of the United Nations, the main efforts at renewal have focused on some aspect of charter change that in turn has usually required some kind of alteration of the Security Council. One of the better-known efforts in that vein was encouraged during the time leading up to the UN's 50th anniversary in 2005, in the report presented by then Secretary-General Kofi A. Annan, titled, "In Larger Freedom."

That report submitted for consideration included upgrades to the charter, changes in the General Assembly and Security Council, and the inclusion of a new Human Rights Council. Odds are you didn't hear anything about this, and for one simple reason: *None* of the recommendations that required charter change happened.

To put it bluntly, no efforts that include charter change have ever come close to seeing the light of day at this or any other time of the UN's history. I suspect this will continue to be the case even as the nature of the threats to international peace and security continue to evolve dramatically.

Let me be quite clear. *Nothing in this book even remotely proposes a charter change.* In fact, until something similar to the social technology proposed here is put into place, charter change and other such institutional maneuvering could be counter-productive to the kind of changes that are needed. Occam's razor is very applicable here: The simpler the solution to the UN's current impasse with regard to involving the tech community on critical cybersecurity issues, the better.

Game-Changer #1
Meta-Nets: A Proven Successful Strategy For Organizational Adaptation

History has proven time and again that small shifts in perspective and calculation can unlock whole new possibilities. Consider Copernicus.

Didn't he look up at the same skies as everyone else? What was the difference that led him to see and report something that amounted to turning the world of his time upside down? By looking through a stronger lens that few had available to them, he made a simple observation of how the planets actually moved—not around the earth, but rather around the sun.

Everyone else who looked up at the sun assumed it was circling the earth. But Copernicus had the clearer, more technologically advanced, point of view. Further, he could prove it mathematically. The earth circled the sun and no matter the resistance to his big idea, the result was a complete reframing of how we look at the heavens, and in so doing, of how we navigate across the earth.

His observation, if you look at it alone, was a relatively small change in perspective, but from that small change came huge leaps forward in every area of human knowledge and experience. Likewise, the approach I am proposing involves small changes in perspective by those who are the major stakeholders in the work of the UN, and by major, I do not only mean the well-known ones such as the Security Council, the Secretary General and the Member States of the General Assembly.

There are many agencies working within and at the UN, comprising the whole picture. Key stakeholders include a multitude of civil society organizations undergirding much of the UN's actual work in the field. All have a great deal at stake in the UN itself, but none of them, by their relative largeness or smallness, or proximity to the more powerful nexus of the UN are exempt from being stuck in pre-existing habits and structures that no longer serve us well.

These small changes can be most simply facilitated by adopting an innovative way of setting up specially tasked small groups, what I call "meta-nets" for two reasons. First, these meta-nets would be convened to focus on specific issues for a designated period of time. They would also be mandated to keep their scope of focus at a global level, i.e., a "meta-humanity" perspective.

"Meta" is a Greek term that has several meanings, but the popular use of it today is usually for something that is "beyond." You see it in listings for academic courses when the topic is about an entire field of study, such as meta-philosophy. Likewise, these small groups at the UN would have the mandate to focus on the issue at hand from a meta-humanity perspective.

Many corporations realize they need to change in order to survive, but they also recognize they cannot change everything all at once. They have to maintain what they've already built, but their conundrum is what to change and how to do it fast enough and strategically enough to fend off irrelevance and death.

Second, these meta-nets would operate much like a social app, a small group within a much larger operating system in the same way that apps work in iPhones or Androids. Meta-nets would enable large organizations such as the UN to better focus existing resources for the development of optimal strategic initiatives around a particular threat.

In speaking of threats, let me quickly address how turning one's perspective from threat to opportunity is essential for not wasting time and energy when solutions to said threats are needed in the most expedient manner. In that regard, the greater the threat, the bigger the opportunity.

In a moment, I will discuss a corporate strategy that uses this concept of big opportunity for corporations facing competitive market threats. These threats are as deadly to corporations as cyber threats are to world peace and security.

Turning from focusing on threats, to working out solutions as a big opportunity is not just about putting on rose-colored glasses. It is about getting down to the real issues at hand without spending inordinate time and resources in figuring out what went wrong. It's about focusing precious and limited commodities on what can be done going forward.

This perspective takes a particular kind of leadership, one that is addressed by the business model I am making applicable for the UN. For that reason, the two kinds of leadership required to work in tandem for these meta-nets to achieve their agenda is addressed separately in Section #2 of this chapter. Suffice it to say, spending time requesting the UN to change its current management process is futile and unnecessary. Daily maintenance and innovation are not mutually exclusive, but it is very difficult for those in charge of the former to put their energy into working out the latter.

Thus, the use of meta-nets at the UN is one way to tackle the many fires that need putting out every day, all over the planet, without having to usurp the UN's management process. Because cybersecurity is one such blaze that could someday exceed anyone's ability to contain, meta-nets would not be asked to envision things for the UN, as there are already enough people engaged in that. Rather, they would be designated to address very specific issues, and be given a fairly tight time frame in which to do so. As with many a global threat, time is of the essence.

In their placement at the UN, each meta-net would be particularized, as all apps are, for their specific focus (threat/

opportunity), their context (<u>ECOSOC</u>, <u>UNODC</u>, Security
Council, General Assembly, etc.), and their time-frame. Just
as an app on our various devices provides a focused use of
their otherwise enormous computing power, meta-nets are
small networks of stakeholders who would come together
from across all levels of the relevant stakeholder groups to
work together for specified time periods.

Apps are incredibly malleable, and usually they are not
expensive. They address a specific need and fill a specific
niche. When they are no longer needed, we easily delete
them and just as easily add another app to do a different type
of task. Meta-nets at the UN would be utilized in a similar
manner. There isn't time to develop an extended program
over a span of years to address many of the global threats
emerging today. Meta-nets would be convened to quickly
create strategic initiatives *on a specified big opportunity*.

They enable nimble responses to critical issues causing
crises. To more fully understand meta-nets and how they
have already been used to help major corporations adapt and
not falter, I strongly suggest you read John Kotter's book
Accelerate.[2] Not that you will find any overt reference to
meta-nets, as meta-nets are my adaptation of what Kotter
refers to as the network side of his dual operating system that
he proposes for the corporate context.[3]

His books are more than informative, and not a difficult
read for any non-corporate person. Kotter is a Harvard
professor in business and economics who created a method

of setting up an internal dual operating system, granting large, well-established, hierarchical organizations a way to deal with rapid, competitive external changes. He used the term, "networking side" to describe this secondary operating system within the larger context of the corporation.

At one period in my career, I was brought in to restructure a company with large assets (literally large, as it was a bus charter and tour company). The company was mid-size, but even so, it was not easy to implement needed changes.

Later, as I better understood Kotter's work, I could more fully understand why many of my efforts to restructure that company were not easily implemented, though everyone agreed changes were sorely needed. Further, because of more than a decade-and-a-half participating at the UN, I could even more readily see how his method could be tweaked and implemented at that body. In both cases, I made progress in many ways, but when it came to more effectively (and quickly) responding to critical issues, in the corporate context and even more so at the UN, I found institutional inertia to be the sticking point.

When I read Kotter's description of large, well established, hierarchical corporations, I could not help but compare them to the UN. Of course like any model, his will need a few tweaks to manage the same effect at the UN. I am not shy to suggest those tweaks, given that many years of participation at the UN afforded me the ability to connect the dots from the business side to what would work in this organization.

The strategic initiatives developed by each meta-net would arise from the work of meta-volunteers who would come from all levels across the system relevant to the opportunity being addressed. I use the term meta-volunteers to differentiate between the so many other kinds of volunteers that work in various capacities at the UN.

What I mean here is that those who apply to join a meta-net team are agreeing to volunteer their time and expertise outside of their normal work as a diplomat, UN staffer, NGO representative or otherwise UN expert. They are the ones that get to innovate on critical and urgent opportunities. They are not paid extra. They want to see this work done and they see it as being within their responsibilities, and so are willing to participate without extra compensation.

Because the team members on the meta-nets come from the UN family of organizations, they know what and how things can and cannot be done. They are not consultants, new hires or appointees brought in from outside the organization, as is often done for strategic change. Therefore they are familiar with the UN and how it all works because that is their daily context.

Once strategic initiatives have been developed by a respective meta-net, they are handed off to the existing structures of the UN system for implementation, and the meta-net then dissolves. Meta-nets do not take over existing

UN management, decision-making or other maintaining responsibilities.

They are volunteer add-ons chosen from every level within the larger family of organizations, stakeholders and invited experts specifically to *accelerate* innovation, find ways to creatively respond to the big opportunities that lie hidden behind some of the largest threats that hierarchies are only able to react to in predictable, and not always appropriate ways. In relation to the Security Council, for example, meta-nets could be actuated via a specific series of Arria-Formula meetings. These meetings are a recent practice providing opportunities for frank but confidential exchanges of views on matters of concern, and they can include non-State parties[4].

Toward A Meta-Humanity Perspective

Meta-nets have two main characteristics that become clearer as they are better understood, and these do require some shifting of perspectives. The first has to do with the meta part. Intentionally, these teams are not formed to address inter-national issues, rather they pertain to meta-humanity concerns to which of course, nations can and must contribute. I make this distinction of meta-humanity because of the confusion we often have about traditional inter-national engagement that is between one or more nations, but has national sovereignty as the base line priority and globally minded international engagement that has humanity as a whole as its baseline priority.

One might ask, "Isn't that the fundamental purpose of the UN?" And the answer would be, "Yes, but not entirely." It's the not entirely that is key here. The UN's members are states. So of course their interests are vital. Everything centers on the negotiations and agreements of these nations that are at best, in the interests of humanity, but not always. We cannot expect Member States to lose their self-interest and capitulate to a meta-humanity perspective in an organization that does not mandate this. It is nevertheless important to understand that agreements between nations do not necessarily champion meta-humanity level interests.

National level and meta-humanity level interests can and will overlap at times, but in the purposes of their work and any decision of the teams, these meta-nets are mandated to decide in the interests of meta-humanity as fully as they are able.

This distinction can also help explain some of the fuzzy logic and consequent fuzzy language that then shows up at the UN, and as I have observed over a span of many years, in almost all international diplomacy. It is one of the shades of gray of which the most seasoned diplomats and politicians often make use to their advantage.

In part it can be best understood as the difference between the spoken language and the body language of the UN. The

UN was founded for the purpose of serving all nations, thus humanity, so of course conversations, resolutions and any language seeking to gain support will endeavor to stir the soul, to uplift and inspire. To do this, it usually draws upon language pertaining to all humanity. The physical counterpart, however, is often not quite so lofty.

The UN's body language of its charter makes it clear that "The Organization is based on the principle of the sovereign equality of all its Members."[5] So structurally, decisions and actions are those of nations, not of social structures designed to represent the interest of humanity. The UN is designed to accommodate the (current193) Member States that have a stake in the overall vision of the UN and in supporting peace, security and development. The Member States are like spokes of a wheel, in this case, leading into and out of the UN hub. Without them, the UN would quickly become an isolated organization with little impact upon the spinning world of international affairs.

Meta-humanity altruism can and does appear at the UN, but the UN Charter does not require it. Not warring is a UN mandate, but this is quite distinct from acting for the benefit of humanity as a whole, for the sake of our meta-humanity.

We humans quickly fall into the patterns of words and phrases that surround us. Member State diplomats and their office core come to the UN with the global view in mind, but again, they are there to represent their sovereign nation's interests. Thus, their thoughts and actions are by nature and by the pressure from their own capitals more often pulled back toward home rather than in the global direction.

It is usually within the context of global level threats such as global warming, global financial crises and so on that there is more of a chance of meta-humanity based decisions being made. A question that then arises from awareness of this tension between the body and the mind of nation-based politics is, "What are we to do?"

"We can't solve problems by using the same kind of thinking we used when we created them."

Albert Einstein

Is there something the UN *can* do, to more systematically devise solutions to global threats that can work? My answer is quite simply, "Yes, indeed." And meta-nets are one of the instruments that can facilitate this.

Do keep in mind that this book is not proposing some new overall vision for the UN, nor is it trying to sell a particular version of peace and security. What it is about, are the steps we can take to turn today's threats and challenges into exceptional opportunities by using the resources and structures the UN already has in place. It is about the UN rising to 21st-century challenges by choosing to adopt new social innovations by leveraging its existing resources differently.

The kind of leadership *United Nations Unlocked* advocates will augment the UN's existing management leadership. It does not require new budgets, rather a different way of utilizing existing resources, much as a new app on your phone helps you utilize the existing computing power of your mobile device for specific purposes. Similarly, meta-nets are a new way to optimize the contribution and strengths of existing UN stakeholders. Again, when facing issues of peace and security leveraged by technology, that part of civil society with a critical role will be the tech community.

Meta-nets will unleash the desire to respond to threats and challenges as opportunities. They will address the inadequacies and weaknesses present in local, national and global systems that resulted in problems growing to their current levels. This leadership initiative is proactive, not locked into victimization and reactive "they did it" leadership. It recognizes life is messy and that we need to get in there and clean it up—fast. It sees the problem as a timely opportunity to create a solution.

By keeping the focus of institutional activity on innovation and solutions and giving the UN a mechanism for this, energy will not be used to resist the faster-moving tech tectonic plate. The real question then becomes, "How quickly can the UN adapt and work with tech leaders and representatives to jump-start innovative global security measures so as to ensure our collective well-being?" The answer is, by allowing them an innovative leadership role within the UN via the installation of meta-nets to create dual, non-competing management and transilient systems.

Game-Changer #2
Major Organizations Need
Two Kinds of Leadership

Having spent many years involved with and developing leadership and capacity building courses, as well as taking the lead in some innovative initiatives, has provided me with a hands-on understanding of what works, and what to expect when bringing innovation into resistant environments. The term that keeps coming to mind as I have thought about and practiced change leadership is transilience. Transilient leadership by its very nature is innovative. How else are we going to leap across gaps and push into new territories where we have never been before unless we devise something new? Transilient leadership acknowledges the role of innovation and transilient leaders lean into difference and change.

Meanwhile, traditional corporate leaders lean heavily on hierarchical structures and articulated processes. But even here, transilience is needed, if differently than that which is required in a start-up enterprise. While dreamers and visionaries open us to vistas we may not have imagined possible; they often lack the management skills that can bring their ideas to market.

Management leadership is more often taught in MBA courses, based upon that which large corporations traditionally sought. Senior managers are still needed and are still vital to organizations, but we are also entering a phase where the pace of change is creating so many unknowns that even large well-established organizations are now at sea.

They are facing the same kind of unfamiliarity and turbulence that start-ups experience, indicating that corporations, from start-up to well-established, will more and more need transilient leaders who will find the way forward for their organizations, especially in the midst of confusion and disruption. Added to this, globalization and the growing impact of technology on our social systems have had a decentralizing effect, internationally networking our information and economies. The chorus of "better, faster" challenges organizations to more widely and evenly distribute capacities into every part of their structure.

In other words, we are increasingly looking for ways to distribute the function of leadership throughout the entire organization and not just in the hands of an elite few. Transilient leadership is attuned to this trend and when combined with suitable social mechanisms, becomes a new and compelling option for organizational change.

Were the UN to couple transilient leadership with a mechanism such as meta-nets, it will transform, simply by the very act of doing so. Access to previously underutilized energies, insights, and leadership capacities, from the Secretary-General, Under-Secretary-Generals, diplomats on down to coordinators and participating NGO representatives, will make the daily business of the organization hum—and at an octave higher.

As defined, transilience is the ability and capacity to leap across gaps or to move from one place to another. Transilient leadership is the ability and capacity to lead others in this process of innovation and change. It means having the foresight, intent and capacity to take a leap and go somewhere new, and to create the vehicles others need to get there. Transilient leaders, aware of the differences that create the gaps in our thinking, our structures and our processes work to find ways to bridge the resistance that difference creates and more, values difference as the source of latent energy that when tapped, will propel us forward.

Principles of Transilient Leadership

Transilient leadership is guided by a few basic principles. Persistent adaptation of these principles helps keep transilient leaders agile, adaptive, open and confident.

1. Change Is Always Happening: Regardless of how much we may want to keep things the same, nothing will stay the same. Even at the molecular level, there is constant vibration, rotation, and interaction. It happens everywhere. The implications of this principle are that to keep things the same requires as much, perhaps more, effort than to innovate changes. A different kind of effort is required for the latter than the former and the amounts of energy needed are determined by many factors.

This is perhaps most easily understood in the leadership context as the difference between managers and innovators. Both require leadership decisions and the capacity for making those decisions, but the outcomes are different. One is not good nor the other bad. They are different and their appropriateness to the vision of the task at hand will determine the kind of leadership needed.

2. Context Matters. Nothing humans do, especially in a social sense, is done in a vacuum. Each action has a context with a temporal element, an environmental or geospacial element, and implicit or explicit purposes. Then, of course, there are cultural components (usually associated with the environmental/geospacial aspect), proximity to other events and actions and so on. But the main point here is to note that everything, every decision, and every action has a context and so looking at the action alone may provide some insight, but it will be incomplete without understanding the context.

Another critical form of context when we are considering social change is the organizational context. Just as the architecture of a house shapes a person's experience when he or she enters or lives in that house, so do organizational structures extend or limit the capacity to act effectively in society. This latter consideration is often forgotten by many of us when we are busy with our daily endeavors, and organizational structure only becomes more critical when we undertake a social change.

3. Timing Matters. Actions not only take place in certain environments but also at particular times. With the ebb and flow of planetary and social changes, day and night, the seasons, opportune moments come and go making some small actions significant while other, even larger events, get lost in the annals of time. Windows of opportunity do open and new seasons are born, but windows also close, and chances can be lost, sometimes forever.

4. Small Change is Generative. Any change created in one location will make for changes, even if small, everywhere else. The idea of small changes creating larger seemingly unconnected changes was popularized as the butterfly effect. Others have used the pebble in the pond image to indicate our connectedness and impact. Whatever way you prefer to think about it, be it social or physical, every change creates new pressures and influences everywhere else.

Of course, in physical terms, the impact is inversely proportional to the distance from that original place of impact as in the ripples in the pond, so most of the time the differences are negligible. Nevertheless, these changes can accumulate. When these small changes are taken into social environments, in addition to the physical accumulation, psychological drivers also come into play and can further multiply the changes being made.

5. Small Changes Accumulate Into Bigger Changes. Today this is very clear especially in the social media where the Twitter effect can turn unimportant occurrences into mainstream news. There are, of course, socially significant instances where many voices become heard because of this cumulative effect. Whether a particular instance is perceived as good or bad, it remains true that small changes accumulate. In this way, small repeated habits become patterns of behavior that can be played out across organizations and cultures.

6. Cooperation is Inevitable. Putting this very simply, at the planetary level, either we will find ways to cooperate and collaborate or, sooner or later, by some means or another, we will cease to exist. Anything short of extinction then, makes cooperation inevitable. Underlying this principle, therefore, is the assumption that there is some way to cooperate, though we just may not have found it yet.

7. Opportunities Are Impossibilities Reframed. Humans are meaning makers, constructing meaning interactionally with our experience. Just as we can decide a situation is impossible, we can also reconstruct it as an opportunity. That usually takes some effort to change our perspectives and where necessary, our limiting beliefs.

8. People are resourceful. We have all that we need to solve the problems and challenges we face. When we create mechanisms that extend our resourcefulness as individuals to teams and communities, and farther beyond, our scope of impact is likewise leveraged at those levels.

Game-Changer #3
Pivotal Partnership Can Create
Powerful Difference Engines

In essence, what I've proposed thus far is for the UN to establish a security meta-net to assist the Security Council in wrestling with these very complicated global level threats, and thus uncover huge opportunities such as creating security systems heretofore un-envisioned. In Chapter Five, I provide a step-by-step outline as to how such a meta-net might be generated.

In that chapter, I will discuss who would join such a meta-net, what they could be expected to accomplish and more. In so doing, I will further explain the usefulness of these meta-nets and how the UN could benefit beyond the Security Council by implementing them.

Because the concept of meta-nets has yet to be fleshed out, for now, I want to add that their inclusion in the UN system is more like adding breathing space than it is strapping on additional and questionably needed armor.

Then, as we discuss the inclusion of entrepreneurs and experts from the tech world, meta-nets become a natural way to infuse UN thinking with fresh perspectives from a part of society that, like it or not, is restructuring how we engage with our world.

On the tech side, a security meta-net would include a well-chosen group of leading entrepreneurs and cyber specialists. They would bring with them connections to networks that they could plumb when needed to address specifics under the umbrella of whatever big opportunity the meta-net defines.

On the UN side, it would at the very least enable engaged Security Council members and staff to become more aware of the scope of possibilities in providing security innovations at a global level, for the sake of meta-humanity. There would be many side-benefits and secondary impacts from the meta-nets' initiatives, such as the UN being exposed to the agile iterative methods the tech communities use daily, and frankly, take for granted.

Start-up tech companies usually create and work best within environments that are organized to handle threats as opportunities. In other words, they don't wait until the company has a formal management structure to deal with competitive forces. They are from the get-go a flatter, leaner hierarchy, with an "all hands on deck" attitude. The competitive pressures and early phases of development that these start-ups face keep them organizationally nimble.

They constantly need new ideas and new approaches. Waiting for those ideas to go up a corporate ladder and come back down in a formal dictate, after an elongated study, doesn't cut it. Someone else will have already taken their idea and run with it.

In the UN environment, a security meta-net tasked with developing strategic initiatives around a specific set of cyberthreats would be a new way for the considerable knowledge capital of the Security Council to be put to work. I can imagine, and even hope, that some diplomats find their encounters with these innovative minds refreshing and enlivening.

On the other hand, as stated, the tech world is immersed in itself. They are acutely aware of what they and other tech companies are doing, but outside of that, most do not think long or hard about the global level ramifications of the amazing things they do everyday. At the very least, rubbing elbows with diplomats and the like would be enlightening for the tech representatives.

By putting these two divergent groups together, I cannot help but believe that exciting new possibilities would be revealed to both sides involved. I further believe that the synergy of these two dynamic worlds could very well push forward the boundaries of cooperation and thinking in ways currently not envisioned, and as of yet, not made possible.

What are usually lost in mature hierarchical entities are the creative opportunities that lie within the primordial soup phase of an emerging entity. In those early, barely differentiated stages of a start-up's life cycle (they could still be in the garage), the founders are at the center of a network.

In newly emerging corporations, there is little to no hierarchical structure that is typical of established and highly managed organizations. Opportunity seeking and risk-taking are their hallmarks. That's how they seize upon concepts that may be seen by some as useless or offbeat, and yet when tweaked into a simple application, quickly becomes something no one can live without.

The security meta-net would be this kind of undifferentiated network, a team of transilient leaders who feel the urgency of developing solutions, of envisioning possibilities, not wasting time drilling down on problems, their causes and nuances. They would need to summon the intellectual and emotional commitment needed for the task at hand. They would be willing to seek out connections to those in related fields of study and work, while also figuring out how to work with one another. All the while, they would stay focused on developing possible courses of action, exploring how to turn threats into opportunities that could better secure the well being of our meta-humanity.

It would not be a hierarchy with leaders and followers, typical of the UN's current structure. Certainly, on different topics and various occasions, one or two team members might take the helm, but this kind of leadership is fluid and arises when needed by circumstance, not demanded by position. This arrangement would always be flexible. The meta-net team members would be learning how to keep their innovative network side aligned with the UN hierarchy side, but nonetheless maintain their focus on recommending needed changes, commensurate with the challenges presented to them.

It is these kinds of networks that Kotter urges be re-established in mature organizations, so they can remain agile and responsive to the current environment and the incredible pace of change afoot. He warns that not to do so is tantamount to irrelevance or worse. In the business world, continued irrelevance eventually means only one thing, and that is corporate death. The question that begs to be asked then, is what does irrelevance mean for the UN and its future?

Since the idea of a security meta-net may require the tech community to freely give of their time and possibly money, we also have to consider how likely it would be for the tech community to see this as a significant way to contribute and choose to participate.

I have already put my own toe into this water through meetings, discussions and exchanges with executive directors, researchers and consultants. Among the tech institutes I have connected with are the Machine Intelligence Research Institute (MIRI) and the University of Cambridge's Centre for the Study of Existential Risk (CSER), the Association for the Advancement of Artificial Intelligence

(AAAI) symposia, and the Institute of Electrical and Electronics Engineers (IEEE).

As I network and connect with tech experts and specialists in the cybersecurity realms, I continue to find it interesting to note how irrelevant the UN is to their world, even when they deal with internationally launched cyberattacks. The current gap between tech's cyberworld and the bricks and mortar of the UN world is quite staggering, especially in light of their common interest in security, privacy, rights and the social good. If therefore, the international and UN communities see any reason to foster relationships with the tech community, they will need to do something fairly attention grabbing, and even the most attractive offer may need to be reduced to an eight-second sound bite.

To give you a numerical perspective as well as immediate proof of the disconnect between the tech community and the UN, stop reading right now and google the exact phrase "UN and technology" and see how many hits you get. Compare that to when you google "business and technology." For the UN search, you will get 14 or 15 hits; for the business search, you will get a few more — over 87,000,000.

This is no small hitch in this whole proposal and it is also why I spend some time in Chapter Four offering practical steps to getting the proposal underway, but specifically as to how the UN can connect with the tech community. My stint of years at the UN has a payoff here, and it is why I even dared to write this book in the first place. I do believe there is a real way forward. Is that way easy? Perhaps not, but what would it cost to simply consider it? More to the point, what might it cost to not do so?

I suspect that the work of figuring out how to engage, draw in and collaborate with the tech sector will help infuse the UN with what it needs for its longevity and 21st-century relevance. Moreover, at first, it may be hard to find actors in the tech community with sufficient sense of their role as global citizens to be willing to give of their time. But all is not lost. In every sector of human activity, even in the cold, harsh world of competitive commerce, there are those who see the larger picture and feel the pull to work in larger and larger domains and connect to that larger vision where what they do matters to the future of humankind.

I have already met many of these remarkable, bright, young, and a few not so young, inspiring techies. There are signs they could be called upon to genuinely contribute, and many would sincerely appreciate the opportunity. After all, it is just as much their world as it is the UN's at stake.

The UN is not the first organization to have its future threatened by obsolescence and irrelevance. Humans are constantly resurrecting new enterprises out of the dust of companies that have collapsed; however, and I cannot emphasize this enough, the UN is not a widget maker or a soda company. Its demise at this particular juncture of human history would have dire consequences.

Yes, we would go on without it, but to rebuild any semblance of the intricate relationships that the UN has created amongst friendly and hostile nations over the past seven decades would be a herculean effort. We don't have time for the recreation of this institution. We have really and truly meta-humanity level issues to address and resolve. The future of humanity and the planet are being shaped by what we do today.

For the UN to attract and get a response from the tech world will require a willingness on behalf of the UN to embrace innovation from the beginning. Using a blend of transilient leadership and Kotter's business model, tweaked toward meta-nets, makes this doable, as the UN does not need to change itself inside out. It just needs to open a few doors, here and there, and let some fresh air, some new ideas come in.

The next chapter will provide a framework for better understanding leadership and possibly providing you with new leadership intelligence. For example, by parsing out the difference between management-style (maintenance) and difference-oriented (innovative) leadership, you can also better assess leadership needs. Then you can take the appropriate action if either the individuals and mechanisms you have in place are not yet appropriate to the nature and scale of the task.

There are other nuts and bolts when it comes to effecting change, and I've included some of those in the appendices.

They are helpful for the personal and professional levels but are not germane to the organizational scope at which this book is aimed. Let's now engage an outline of leadership using a three dimensional model that serves as a means of assessing what kind of leadership is required to achieve different goals, be they managing or innovating.

CHAPTER THREE
Transilient Leadership:
A 3D Model

While pulling off the covers first thing in the morning, stepping onto the floor and then heading downstairs, I barely give a second thought about the three-dimensional world around me. I am too busy living in it to spend much time thinking about it.

However when I have to replace the overhead light in the bathroom, I do have decisions to make about how to maneuver LED tubes into place, and where to temporarily position delicate light covers, ladders and so on. Momentarily, I need to address some practical questions as to how I'm going to operate in our 3D world. Had I the job of programing a new robot on the Tesla S assembly line, 3D knowledge would definitely be a daily consideration for me.

Similarly, the fact that there are at least three dimensions of leadership are of little interest to most, until they are confronted with the need to improve their own leadership skills or discover they have to better understand others' leadership styles and strengths. This 3D model of leadership gives shape to what for many remains somewhat invisible and thus provides a way to measure and scale what was previously not measurable.

Whether you are aware of your existing leadership theory, be it trait, behavioral, contingency or power and influence based, these three dimensions provide a new level of leadership intelligence that can be quickly put to use. It can also help you better assess if there is a need for changes to, or adaptations of, your organization's leadership approach, its structures or practices in light of whatever issue you have in mind. These leadership insights will also help you better strategize, plan and implement.

The Three Dimensions of Transilient Leadership

Before I delve more deeply into each dimension of the model, let me provide you with a quick glance as to what each of these three axes represent. Then, you'll have these synopses in mind as we explore each axis on the model.

Difference: This axis provides a way to scale how whether the leadership is forward, solution-oriented, innovative or at the other extreme, backward, insular and at its worse, destructive. In more traditional leadership terms, this axis puts innovation in the positive direction and maintenance or management of current systems and processes closer to the zero or present locus. Destructive leadership is that which pulls backward, undermining existing structures and creating constrictive systems within which there is little to no room for difference or innovation.

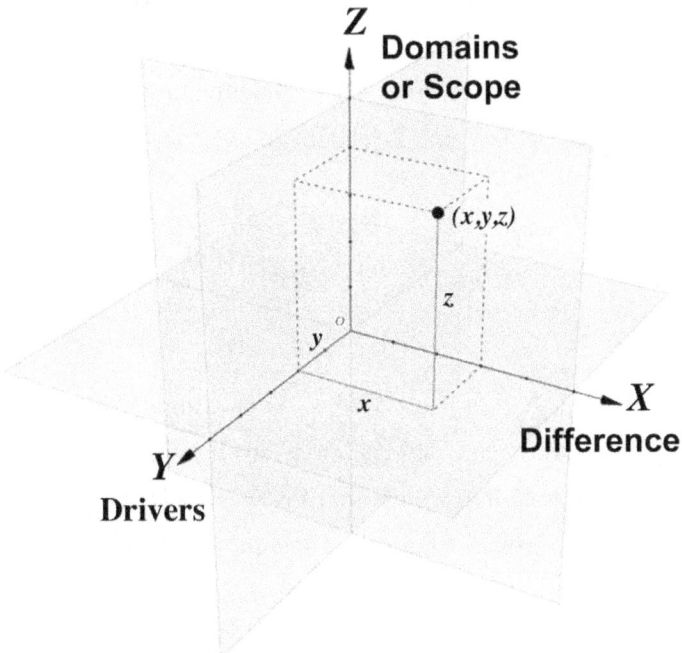

Drivers: This axis allows us to assess which part(s) of the human brain is (are) underpinning our decision-making process. It helps us gauge what aspect of our mind: instinctual, emotional and/or rational, is driving us as we perceive threats and engage opportunities that have compelled us to consider a change.

Domain or Scope: This axis allows us to examine the context and level of human interaction in which we want to effect change, from individual to group to institutional and at times, as far reaching as a meta-humanity effort. Scope considers our sphere of influence and so helps us better see what is needed to complete the changes or management successfully.

The diagram below provides a 3D depiction of that which comprises these X, Y and Z-leadership axes.

X-Axis: Difference

A primary duty of leadership is to make things happen. When done well, leadership is like a lens turning the energies of those involved into a pinpoint of power. Leadership also needs to orchestrate maintenance, health, and well-being.

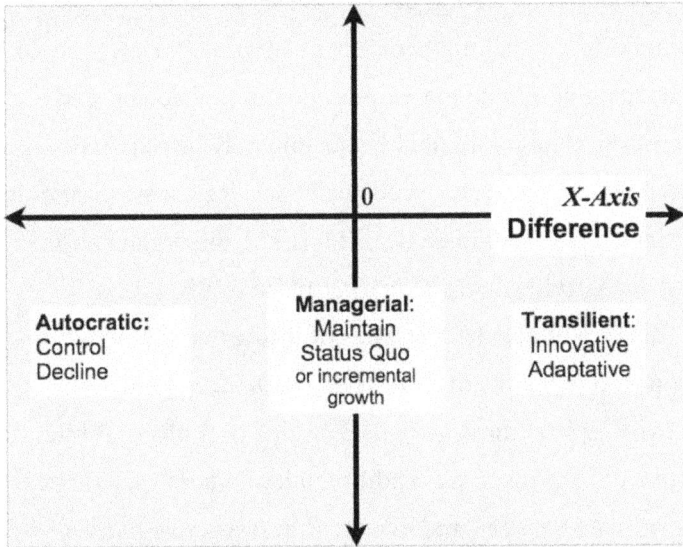

	0	X-Axis Difference →
Autocratic: Control Decline	**Managerial:** Maintain Status Quo or incremental growth	**Transilient:** Innovative Adaptative

This X-axis identifies the difference-making attributes of leadership. That is, it maps out the kinds of difference being sought or pursued. For example, if the specific objectives were the more traditional refinements of an existing system, then a management style of leadership would be chosen.

Of course, even within typical management, significant overhauls may be required with accompanying project management demands, new hires, different forms of financial support and the like. But in the bigger picture of organizational change, this would, in fact, remain solidly within the scope of traditional management style leadership. This kind of difference would lie somewhere on the X-axis closer to the zero point of stability than being further out toward innovation.

For example, should circumstances arise upsetting the calm norm, by making business-as-usual no longer tenable in a changing global marketplace, a more visionary and therefore, change-oriented leadership may be required. To stay relevant, very new products or services or ways of doing business may need to be devised. If not, the organization may face irrelevance and market-place death.

There will also be instances of leadership that work in the negative realms of difference where deconstruction of existing structures and relationships take place. While politics is one place we readily think of where such tactics are utilized between and even within respective parties, no organization is immune to backward thinking reactive leadership.

Why leaders sometimes goes off in such destructive tangents can be partially explained in the next axis where we take a look at somewhat hidden drivers within the human brain that can cause us to react in negative ways that are otherwise inexplicable.

The main point of this axis is to indicate that leadership styles will differ with different degrees of change needed. So for example, maintenance may be more what is required for a particular project, but something more radical and innovative might be needed when larger changes are considered.

Y-Axis: Drivers

The Y-axis adds significant depth when used in conjunction with the other two axes that enrich our understanding of leadership capacities.

This dimension helps us understand how we can end up with a continuum of leadership types that range from brutal tyrants to non-engaged authoritarian styles to fully interactive constructive, innovative leaders.

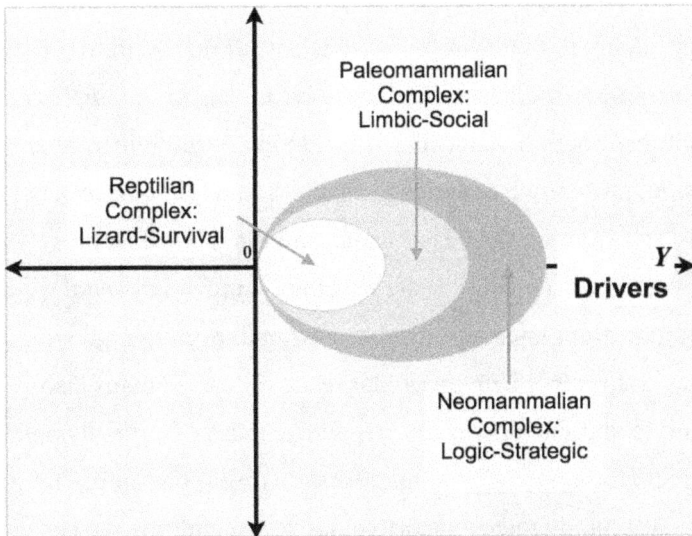

The motivations that drive us lie deep within our brains, and these depths evolved in a somewhat layered way over time in response to the challenges humans have faced. The oldest part of our brain, as proposed by the American physician and neuroscientist Paul D. MacLean in 1990, is referred to as the reptilian or lizard brain, centers on survival and gives rise to our fight and flight responses.

No part of our brain ever shuts off, so when we first hear about some change coming down the pipeline, our initial reaction often carries with it some form of resistance. That is the lizard brain sending signals to be on guard as the unknown might be dangerous, because, for millions of years and even today, lack of knowledge can imperil us.

However, humans are not merely instinctual beings. We also developed social skills and without them, we would very likely not be here today. This part of our brain, where we connect to others in collaborative endeavors to improve our chances of a better life, is located in our limbic system. Here is where we experience a fuller range of emotions, not just gut reaction fear. That is why, although we encounter new things on a daily basis, we quickly move beyond a fight or flight knee jerk reaction. Instead, even though we may at first feel a tingle of that reactive fear, humans also tend to approach the unknown with a sense of curiosity and anticipation. Part of that interest stems from our ability to socialize and create supportive networks, and this lessens our personal risk, which makes the future quite less intimidating. Thus, we are willing to investigate new possibilities to make progress.

Much later, the human brain developed the neocortical system where reasoning and logic reside. It typically takes

0.7 seconds for our brain to react to a dangerous situation. It will take a bit longer to sort through emotions that help us connect and collaborate with others. Compared to these two processes the thinking part of our brain is relatively slow.

In other words, the brain first reacts, then feels, and finally puts a thought together. Because the thinking part is what occurs last, and takes the longest, we pay more attention to it than the older, deeper layers of the brain. The Cartesian thesis, "I think therefore I am" may be more than a bit misleading. It would be more accurate to say, "I react, then feel and finally rationalize that reaction and feeling, and therefore I am."

If we only attribute everything we do to reason and logic, we readily fool ourselves. As I studied these three aspects of the human brain lizard (reptilian brain), limbic (paleomammalian brain) and logic (neomammalian brain), I also recognized them as three motivational drivers of how we operate. They became a quick way to better assess the part of the brain driving me hardest, as well as somewhat figure out what was driving those with whom I was interacting. Getting a better picture of what is going on with ourselves or others, when it comes to these drivers does not necessarily remove one's frustration when others are speaking in reasonable terms (logic), but acting in reactive ways (lizard). Nonetheless, it does help to notice which driver is dominant in those with whom we have dealings.

Here are the correlatives that are helpful when assessing what's going on that may be enhancing progress or giving rise to counter-productive behaviors:

L1: The Lizard (reptilian) brain - S1: Survival mode of the R-complex.[6]

L2: The Limbic (paleomammalian) brain - S2: Social, feeling mode of the limbic system.

L3: The Logic (neomammalian) brain - S3: Strategic, thinking mode of the cerebral neocortex.

Likewise, just as there is no right or wrong about the X-axis difference continuum, neither is there a right or wrong about which driver dominates. All drivers are at play all the time, but one usually takes an edge, then recedes while another takes over, and so forth. Let's unpack this dynamic a little more to see how it might work first for a person whose motivations hover mainly around their lizard region.

It is helpful to keep in mind that emotions play a significant role in decision-making and this has become clearer with the paradigm shift in decision theory in the last few decades.[7] This is why marketing works, and why the best marketers include scarcity, fear of loss, guilt and or aversion to regret.

The primacy of their reactionary survivalist lens does not mean they will not exhibit any logic or compassion. Survivalist concerns, however, ensure the correlative emotions of fear, guilt, and regret will be present in their conversations, their rhetoric, and even their vision of the future. If this person then also uses their social skillfulness and logic to powerfully motivate others and align them with this survivalist, reptilian approach, you can begin to imagine the possible dangerous scenarios arising.

They could become the kind of activist who will advocate for expedient (violent) means to achieve their ends. Their rhetoric will also probably intentionally emphasize their listeners' L1 centers, eliciting strong survivalist reactions and fear. When we are ignited along these lines, social connectivity and strategic thinking are narrowed into exclusivist, protectionist perspectives and stances.

Vice-versa, someone who understands that we all want to survive and even thrive, but balances this with limbic compassion and social inclusivism, is the kind of person we want to have as a team member or even better, as a coach of the team. These are just two opposite ways that drivers interplay to give rise to our reactions, feelings and thoughts.

Of course, we are all more complicated than the above depictions. In general, which is all that this graph can provide us, it is useful to know when we are reacting, consolidating collaborative relationships, or developing a strategy that requires us to slow down and allow our brain time to sift through complex thoughts and multiple options.

There is one more continuum germane to the call to action in this book, and it has to do with the scope of our impact and influence. Let's now take a brief look at the third axis.

Z-Axis: Scope

This Z-axis measures the scope of possible actions ranging from internal self-awareness to family, public, corporate/community, national, global and meta-humanity levels of social organization. Again, this dimension of leadership does not imply that any one part of the Z-axis is an ultimate place of residence, so to speak. Rather it shows us the full range of places we can visit—and need to—as leaders.

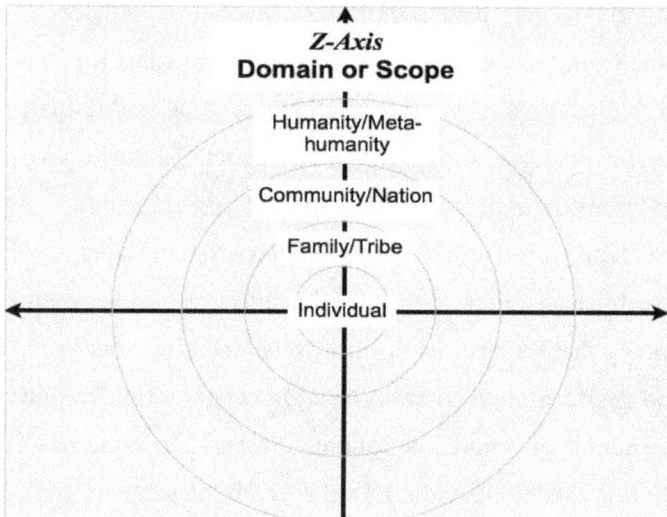

Z-Axis
Domain or Scope

Humanity/Meta-humanity

Community/Nation

Family/Tribe

Individual

Having this Z-axis as a dimension of leadership helps us notice the level at which we are functioning. If the X-axis gives us a difference length, that is looking toward innovation or looking backward to older more stable, sustaining structures, and the Y-axis provides us with depth, the Z-axis affords us height.

How might this help create the clarity focus needed for a team to stay on track? For example, a diplomat or NGO representative who serves at the UN, and is therefore mandated to keep his/her nation's/organization's interest in mind, may be invited to join a team that needs national/expert insights. If that team is then charged with creating strategies to effectively respond to real impacts of global warming, regardless of the national or organizational level interests, can those team members genuinely function at the meta-humanity level? Are they betraying their nation or organization if, by their experience, enhanced by new considerations implicit at the meta-humanity level, they come to conclusions that seemingly contradict the interests of their country or organization?

I will not decide another's moral obligations here. I only want to walk you through this to show how understanding levels scope and spheres of influence can at least inform the discussion and provide additional clarity. This axis then helps us to observe whether we have appropriately adopted plans or suggested strategies for use at the corporate or governmental level that, while they may have worked at the agency level or other levels, are less appropriate or simply won't work in a larger context.

Conversely, some things that work at the global scale may generate real headaches at the national level, hence the cause of many a conundrum at the UN. It also helps us understand why some people don't see an issue with some initiatives because they haven't considered all levels of impact.

Summary

Awareness of where we or others are along any or all of these three axes helps us gauge whether we are engaged in innovation or maintenance of the status quo; choosing a smaller or larger context and scope; or being driven by our lizard-survival, limbic-social, or logic-strategic part of the brain.

You may even be able to watch political elections with new eyes as you assess each politician's locus along these three dimensions of leadership. Which area of your brain are they attempting to motivate and activate? What is the scope of their concern? Are they presenting something new and moving the line forward, or do they want to take you back to the good old days, as if it were possible to live in the past!

Again, there are no right or wrong places on these axes, but there are better fits for the tasks at hand, and this information is valuable. Understanding where we are on each axis takes away a lot of the guesswork when endeavoring to craft a solutions-oriented strategy that will advance the goals that we, and our colleagues, actually want.

Today we can see in many of the political dramas around the world the tensions that arise between reactionary survivalism, social compassion and empathy, and the need for calm, thorough, strategic thinking. We also see the conflict between scopes of concern giving rise to phenomena such as violent extremism cloaked in religious garb.

The tragic fallout comes to us in images of thousands of desperate refugees that depict an increasing global uncertainty. Our fast-changing environment makes it easy for reactive leaders to emerge, appealing to our hidden fears that perhaps the future does not bode well and maybe we should return to a time when things seemed more secure and opportune.

It is harder to move beyond reactions and fears, to slow down just enough with fellow human beings to create more compassionate and rational approaches to the threats that challenge us globally. It may take some time, but it can take much less than we might tend to think.

One way we can shorten the time it takes to get to those rational solutions is to spend less time ruminating over the problems themselves. I would say that enormous amounts of time and effort are wasted both on poorly constructed solutions and half-hearted efforts that fail to inspire and get people and their organizations to the goals they want. It is because while we make resolutions and determine to do something about a crisis, we often continue to point fingers and find scapegoats, and in doing so, sap the energy and will of all involved to move forward.

Even so, there is good reason to believe that the targets we believe would take a miracle to reach may be more attainable than we dare allow ourselves to think. The crux of the matter is simply, what will we allow ourselves to dare to think?

The premise of this book is that while these times are urgent, it is important to take a moment to take a breath from our busy-ness to make more strategic meta-decisions. Taking a break to assess our coordinates in this 3D leadership model provides a baseline position from which we can determine a course through the turbulent waters of our time. Knowing our objective and identifying as accurately as possible where we are now, automatically makes it much clearer for us to determine a way forward.

For the UN, reassessing its position and setting its course heading into the future is akin to a wise captain checking and rechecking the course of his or her ship when making its way through troubled seas.

CHAPTER FOUR
5 Steps to Unlocking the United Nations

In chapter two, I introduced what I consider a critical initiative that the UN's Security Council could incorporate to kick-start a season of innovation at the UN: Create a security meta-net to work in concert with the Security Council on strategic big-opportunity cybersecurity initiatives.

I then reviewed three interlocking ideas that when taken together can be game-changers for the UN:

1. Engaging in organizational adaptation by utilizing meta-nets as simple, doable and practical alternatives to charter change or Security Council reform.
2. Initiating a pivotal partnership between the tech community and the Security Council.
3. Fostering two kinds of leaders and leadership at the UN: Management and Transilient.

From there, I presented a brief, but in-depth explanation of three dimensions of leadership that help to assess where we are in terms of management or innovation. This provided some background as to why the UN and tech communities are quite disparate in their perspective, scope and areas of brain involved, and how transilience could help them become a dynamic match for one another.

A good match

The tech community has strong transilience vectors and the advantages are obvious, enough for the Security Council to deeply consider bringing in such leaders to join specific Security Council related meta-nets and task them with developing innovative solutions for complex cybersecurity related issues. Additionally the (relative) chaos of an unstructured, yet networked, team would be able to pull in a broad spectrum of expertise to innovate effective initiatives, while, as I emphasized, it does not compete with the existing UN hierarchy, an already aptly managed and well-oiled machine.

These meta-nets enable existing structures such as the Security Council to more quickly and accurately respond when faced with newly emergent threats for which it currently has a less than adequate coping mechanism. Engaging some of the tech-best in a security meta-net would provide the Security Council a built-in means to develop outside-the-box strategies. The tech community is used to being tapped for high security profile projects. Why shouldn't the Security Council also tap a group of energized, inspired, diverse and knowledgeable stakeholders to wrestle together to envision change initiatives?

Having these meta-nets at their discretion to tackle critical threats and offer effective ways to perceive such threats as opportunities to make the planet a safer and more secure place for all its inhabitants, is nothing other than a win-win-win situation. It's a win for the Security Council; a win for the tech community; and a win for the Member States to further their work toward a less violent world.

The UN community stakeholders have strong scope vectors in their leadership repertoire, to which the tech community, by and large, has marginal awareness and connection. The tech community is in reality, heavily focused on the more personal realms. Yes, their products impact things far afield, and many do have a passion to make the world a better place, but they tend to have little experience with the socio-political implications of their work.

Their drivers are heavily weighted in the L3 logic-S3 strategic realm and are often missing the L2 limbic-S2 social connector aspect. They may not want to harm the planet, but that is passive stance, very different from being driven to provide direct benefits to all humankind in a comprehensive manner. These differences between the tech and the UN communities are not necessarily bad. Rather, I see the differences as those which can make them good partners to wrestle with both sides of solutions to specific threats, the tech side and the humanity side.

As noted, many in the tech community have simply not activated their global citizen muscles. They haven't had a gut-level epiphany connecting them to a meta-humanity sensibility, even when their efforts cumulatively impact our global community. The relatively isolated incubators in which they work (today's ivory towers) are good for tech development, but do not necessarily connect them to how their results affect human lives and social institutions the world over. So in reality, their focus remains largely on that which affects their ability to think, create and get their software, hardware, or both, into the hands of hopefully delighted consumers.

The UN community provides a counterbalance to this smaller-scope focus. First, the Member State representatives maintain at least a national level point of view, which at specific times can be kicked into a higher gear, such as when they jointly respond to natural disasters. Those in the Secretariat, the General Assembly or ECOSOC look at each issue, word and initiative with an eye on all of the UN's 193 member states, which is in essence a consistent global view.

Compared to almost every organization within the private sector, the UN affords a perch with a view of the world like no other institution, anywhere. Even when diplomats convey their national level concerns cloaked in global sounding words, they are still in an environment where they feel the pressure of meta-humanity issues. How to increase this meta-humanity effect is part of the challenge of the UN, and one small way to accomplish this would be through the implementation of meta-nets.

As tech representatives would come and go at the UN with the formation of various meta-nets in response to specific kinds of cyberthreats, they leave impressions of behaviors that help to foster creative innovation for UN participants to consider in other official contexts. And, these techies would go back into their world with a larger scope of view, perhaps engendering conversations with their colleagues as to how their products could have a more conducive meta-humanity impact. In this way, threads of a very new kind of social fabric would be woven back and forth between the UN and the tech community.

Pulling together or everyone going their way?

Some of today's tech-savviest innovators have issued warnings, put millions into making technology more human-friendly and are positioning themselves to taking their own practical steps for self- and global-protection. For example, visionary and billionaire Elon Musk very recently announced his plan to intensify focus on developing an Interplanetary Transport System (ITS), an action that has already been likened to a modern-day Noah's Ark. What is the average person to make of this?

Is Musk the only one up the hill who has an eye on the wave that is surging toward us *and* who knows he must somehow light a fire of urgency for those of us in the village below? My naive altruistic brain wants to believe that we just have to speak to the global citizen in each of us and at least an adequate number of listeners will respond to the call. But I also know how prevailing and entangled are our L1 and L2 drivers that keep our focus narrowed onto our daily bread, our families, our work and immediate social circles.

In other words, we may indeed want all of humankind to do well, but at the base of every human brain is the part that insists we first get what we need to survive: food, shelter, and so forth. As psychologist Abraham Maslow observed, when we feel secure about basics for ourselves and immediate others, we can then afford to expand the boundaries and scope of our concern, unless we are already keyed into a meta-humanity sensibility. Constant maintenance of a meta-humanity conscience is a lofty plateau we more ordinary folk reserve for saints, but even they would demure at having consistency in that regard.

All this is another way of noting that intentionally creating meta-humanity level thinking and doing does require some effort. The image I have of this comes from energetic states in atoms. When there is the right kind of energy input, electrons will jump to a higher shell.

Likewise, we tend to be energized sufficiently to jump up to higher levels of action and scopes of influence when the environment becomes, shall we say, agitated.

When our socio-political environment heats up, we agitated human equivalent of electrons at least have the UN as a place to address our larger concerns, but where does the UN turn when it needs to jump to the next level? When the world agitates through terrorist attacks, civil wars and demographic upheavals spawning refugees worldwide, where does the UN turn for answers and solutions?

These meta-nets provide that mechanism to which it can turn when its existing structure is maxed out, so to speak. Especially for emerging threats, this mechanism can help key stakeholders from all levels of the organization, work together as partners to devise creative new options that would simply otherwise not exist.

Obfuscation and Self-Sabotage

Before the final section, on the five steps to unlocking the UN, I want to give this last caution since even the most well-intentioned of us will at times obfuscate and self-sabotage. These qualities are not weaknesses, nor evils of humanity. They emerge because of human nature and are idiosyncrasies of the human brain. We just don't always see things within us, and therefore around us, as clearly as we might think, or even want. Objective self-reflection is an acquired skill, at which some people are more adept than others.

Being aware of the integrated yet variably prioritized functioning of our three brains helps us better understand the complexity arising from these often invisible drivers in our lives. We are all three: reactionary and survivalist, caring and social, calculating and reasonable, and usually with varying combinations of all three.

Moreover, while it may be easier to think that reason drives us, we only have to look at what is happening around the world and we can see that reason is only part of why and how we act. Sadly, reason is often used in an artful, passionate and regrettably persuasive way to convince our selves and others that actions driven by lower parts of the brain are the only viable available. What else explains the irrationality of war, something always rued in the aftermath, but so difficult to deter in the buildup phase?

When we stop to think about it, it simply makes sense that the rapid rate of change in our globalizing world brings with it an unpredictability that unsettles us and agitates our lizard brains. With so little remaining the same for long, at some level of our being, we feel the proof of threats everywhere.

These days, if you leave your computer untouched for a few weeks, when you return to it, you may discover it has automatically updated its operating system. If the update turns out to be a major operating system update, the upgrade feels as if *everything* has changed.

Of course not everything has changed, but when the user-interface changes its look and feel, then yes, we feel the change! When so much of our sense of normalcy and non-threat comes from familiarity, it should be no surprise that our lizard brains are more often triggered in today's fast-paced times.

Even when we don't change our personal gizmos all that much, businesses do, governments do, larger technologies do, and so everyone is a part of this tech-driven tidal shift, willingly or not. Underpinning almost everything these days is a pervasive sense of shift and change, and this overtly or otherwise impacts our lizard driver.

Therefore, with the increased levels of exposure to minor and major threats that we experience via technology these days, many of us are functioning on elevated levels of readiness more and more often. Knowing this means that we may need reminders to exercise our focus on strategic issues beyond our survivalist scope of concern. Reacting to every new issue with our lizard brain aroused tends to make us suspicious, even when there isn't a compelling reason to be so.

Understanding the instinctive primacy and pull of our survivalist lizard brain that is typically wary of change and difference, helps us understand why there are strong voices against change of any kind. That strong innate desire for safety and stability shows up as resistance to change in the boardrooms of commerce, politics, religion and society, as well as in the news, in our homes and on the streets.

Just as we have DEFCON (DEFense CONdition) levels for assessing nuclear and similar levels of threat, we might consider monitoring how people react to new technologies and other global changes with perhaps a PERCON (PERson CONdition) scale. Now I'm not entirely serious here, but when it comes to our capacity to misinterpret conversations and stand in the way of progress, even when it does make good sense for all of us, we humans seem to have an endless supply of suspicion.

Going forward then, let's just note that we have this remarkable propensity to obfuscate and self-sabotage from the personal to meta-humanity level. It is no small thing to notice, however, and to take into consideration as we plan for our future. This heightened awareness of how we are actually functioning as individuals and groups can help us better assess where we are and the directions we need to take.

Scene setting for a scenario

This following segment is a collage of events, reports, and existing initiatives taking place within the larger United Nations family of organizations as part of its efforts associated with cybersecurity. These are by no means an exhaustive reiteration of the work of the UN as it relates to cybersecurity, but it does provide some sense of what is being done and how it is going about this work.

This is intended to help set the scene for the 5 Steps I will outline. So please bear with me in these sections where the text gets a little thick with some UN terminology.

1. **ECOSOC** special event entitled "Cybersecurity and Development"[8] held at UNHQ 9th December 2011. At this gathering, the President of ECOSOC, H.E. Mr. Lazarous Kapambwe chairing the event pressed, "We have agreed that cybersecurity is a global issue that can only be solved through global partnership. It affects all of our organizations...and the United Nations is positioned to bring its strategic and analytic capabilities to address these issues."

2. **General Assembly 2013: A/68/98:** Pursuant to paragraph 4 of General Assembly resolution 66/24, a Group of Governmental Experts on Developments in the Field of Information and Telecommunications in the Context of International Security was convened during the General Assembly's 66th Session. Their report was submitted to the 68th Session in A/68/98. Building on the outcomes of an expert group that concluded its work in 2013 A/68/98[9] in the recent 70th Session of the General Assembly, there is another call to convene a group of

governmental experts, on "developments in the field of information and telecommunications in the context of international security."[10]

3. **General Assembly 2015**: A/70/174: pursuant to paragraph 4 of General Assembly resolution 68/243, a second Group of Governmental Experts on Developments in the Field of Information and Telecommunications in the Context of International Security was convened and their findings presented to the 2015 General Assembly in A/70/174.

4. **UNODC & UNICRI**: United Nations Interregional Crime and Justice Research Institute (UNICRI) is doing its best to address many issues including cybersecurity and technology misuse and trains interested Member States on various aspects of this and related issues when those Member States request technical assistance.

5. **Security Council**: It is interesting to note that the Security Council has no references to "cyber" even in more general discussions of international peace and security, in any of its 2015 and 2016 resolutions, or its 2014-2015 Report of the Security Council (2015 – 2016 Report is not out yet). This does not mean the UN as a whole is disregarding the issue as cybersecurity is being addressed through other channels and agencies including the International Telecommunications Union (ITU),

the UN's specialized agency for information and communication technologies – ICTs. However, it does show the Security Council is not addressing that cyberwarfare in any significant way. This means there remains a huge, and perhaps enormously urgent, opportunity for the SC to step up.

6. **Arria-Formula Meetings**: As mentioned back in Chapter two, there is a precedent for the Security Council to conduct very informal meetings and to determine its own practices. The Arria-Formula indicates the latitude available and a good format through which to explore the potential of meta-nets in the Security Council context.

7. **International Telecommunications Union**: The ITU is considered the premier global forum through which parties work toward consensus on a wide range of issues affecting the future direction of the ICT industry. They produce the Global Cybersecurity Index, and provide a framework of 5 pillars for its work: Legal measures; Technical and Procedural Measures; Organizational Structures; Capacity Building and International Cooperation. Through these pillars they grapple with the challenges of integrating international legal issues, cooperation and the like.

8. **UN Development Programme (UNDP)**: UNDP, when asked, will provide cybersecurity technical expertise and advice based on local contexts.

The 5 Steps that Unlock

To this point, I have outlined why the UN and the tech community need to work together and have provided reasons why each one is a good counterbalance for the other. I also introduced three axes of leadership that we need to consider when we assess where we are, in either maintaining structures or leading change in the organization. I also briefly noted some of the more complex issues that arise from underlying dynamics of the three drivers within the human brain.

Putting all this information together, we now come to the essential part where we can take a tour, step by step, of how we can begin to unlock the UN. Here is where the pragmatic person can take heart and more fully engage the intention of this book.

Step 1: The UN pulls the trigger on innovation

The UN is ground zero for UN change. The UN Secretary-General is one first and obvious choice for boldly jump-starting the process of adopting meta-nets within the UN system, though others could do so as well within the scope of their various arenas of responsibility. For example, the UNODC's Director General could initiate such networks to operate on any stalled efforts of UNODC's three operational pillars[11] or its work with the four pillars of the UN Global Counter-terrorism strategy.[12]

The point here is that there is room for adoption of innovation almost anywhere in the UN system, not only on security issues. However I am honing in on the pivotal area of cybersecurity and advancing technologies. I am doing so to stimulate conversation of meta-nets as an innovation for addressing the challenging overlap of terrorism and cyberintelligence, while the issue remains critical, but not yet a full meta-humanity crisis.

Let's now examine more specifically, in five steps, what forming a meta-net would look like in conjunction with the Security Council and cybersecurity issues.

Scenario Sequence 1

One of the Member States on the Security Council, who is coming up for its rotation as monthly president, notices the link between the idea of meta-nets and the recommendation in para. 31 of General Assembly resolution A/70/174 that states:

> "31. While States have a primary responsibility for maintaining a secure and peaceful ICT environment, effective international cooperation would benefit from identifying mechanisms for the participation, as appropriate, of the private sector, academia and civil society organizations."

They decide that during the month of their presidency of the Security Council to utilize the meta-net mechanism during a series of Arria-Formula meetings over the course of the month. Knowing that the Security Council, according to Article 29 of the Charter of the UN, could establish a subsidiary organ on a more permanent basis, the Member State will keep this in mind throughout the meta-net exercise and if progress seems very hopeful, may encourage discussion in this direction. But for now, using the Arria-Formula will be sufficient.

This Member State's Mission to the UN (for ease of reference throughout this scenario, I will refer to the initiating member state as IMS) then begins developing some broad brush-stroke ideas regarding what they consider some of the more significant upcoming threats to international peace and security. This they know to be beyond the current focus and capacity of any UN or UN agency department.

They choose cybersecurity as their focus. They can see the writing on the wall with respect to emerging threats in cybersecurity. After all, it has already been six years since the Stuxnet attack when centrifuges in Iran were hacked with a virus. Consider that six years in tech development years is like twenty years or more in other types of advancements. Further consider that cyber attacks reach beyond computer encased realms to affect physical objects. From computer hacking comes cyber-physical attacks that impact real machines and from there, real lives.

What will cyber attacks look like in one more year? With technical evolution and impact increasing more exponentially than linearly, the IMS is both fascinated and rather horrified by the possibilities all at once—especially because one member of the team has also heard about the new field of smart and autonomous systems, known as Intelligent Physical Systems (IPS) making headway in the artificial intelligence world.

These are intelligent systems embedded in machinery are cognizant, task-able, reflective, ethical, and knowledge-rich. That is, IPS will be aware of their capabilities and limitations, leading to long-term autonomy requiring minimal or no human operator intervention. They will include, but not be limited to, robotic platforms and networked systems that combine computing, sensing, communication, and actuation.

Putting it simply, the IMS can see that the security threats that already include election security, along with computer and data security in general, are at issue. Add to this the fact that most of the Security Council members' own nations are already fully engaged in cyberwarfare and just not talking about it is a huge issue. If nothing changes, how will the Security Council be the one hope for humanity to avoid the scourge of cyber-impacted war?

This IMS has consistently championed meta-humanity causes and knows this rare opportunity as president of the Security Council could be the one window of opportunity they will have until the next time, which may be too late. Emerging threats will not only disturb society by the simple fact of how different they are from the past, but also as tools that unscrupulous non-state actors are more than ready to put to use for their twisted and definitely not meta-humanity purposes.

This brave, but dangerous new world needs proactive efforts made by those with meta-humanity at heart and not just national or lesser interests. So the team gathers their gumption and decides to jump in. What other choice do they have? Do nothing?

Step 2: Clarify big strategic opportunities

The unambiguous strategic changes that already lie within the current scope of the UN are not under discussion. Because the financial implications of meta-nets are also minimal, only engaging volunteers, within and outside of the UN, there is little that could be lost and so very much to be gained by taking up this initiative.

What are being handed over to the meta-net for its attention are high-stakes issues currently beyond the scope and capacity of any existing part of UN organization and the Security Council. The meta-net is charged then to address the threat at hand, find within it strategic opportunities and return their recommendations for action back to the Security Council in an expedient manner, not hastily, but not slowly percolating over them either.

These strategic opportunities are solutions-oriented reformulations of emergent threats for which the UN is not currently equipped to address. Strategic opportunities will be different for each UN department, council, agency or section. Some sections of the UN may have no strategic opportunities to address and their work can continue to be managed through improvements in their existing structure, no meta-nets needed.

The important point to understand here is that the meta-net is to be specifically tasked with developing or innovating toward big opportunity formulations of a specific threat or challenge and not just reactions to the threat. This requires bigger-picture thinking, the incorporation of meta-humanity perspectives and it is this big picture that both galvanizes the team and allows better outcomes to be realized more quickly. Once possible innovations are made clearer, in relation to the threat, the actions put into place and the outcomes they generate can then ripple out to larger and larger spheres, with continued assistance from the meta-net.

Scenario Sequence 2

The IMS is becoming more determined to get ahead of the all but inevitable fall-out from cybersecurity. They can see that putting it on the agenda is less and less of an option. It is urgent and the Arria-formula gives them some room to initiate a meta-net endeavor. The IMS is convinced that they would rather be proactively wrestling with issues of how to do something that hasn't been done before than wait until there is a devastating fall-out. They also talk among themselves as to how things could have gotten this far and realize that humans everywhere procrastinate, even on life threatening issues.

The long and short of this is that the IMS is grappling with seeing the big opportunity that cybersecurity issues are presenting. They begin talking among themselves in new ways, over coffee or tea, in quiet conversations in private about what might be the big opportunity here. They are more and more determined to find something that will help them have a much better grasp of what the possibilities might be. They also realize they need to better understand the latest developments in cyber security.

Knowing that the P5 governmental experts on the issue, (USA's DARPA or Homeland Security, a department in Russia's FSB or China's Cyberspace Administration) will be limited in how they can speak about what they think is possible, the IMS will seek more independent perspectives from those in research and development spheres. Having experts with fewer political constraints engage in the brainstorming, and open discussions will help provide a better grasp of what is coming and how to turn threats into urgently needed and wanted big opportunity.

Of course, for each person involved, there will be security and non-disclosure issues for Member States, the UN and the tech companies involved, but there are sufficient numbers of tech experts from which to draw.

The IMS begins to use their contacts to reach out to start conversations with experts in the field of cybersecurity, intelligent systems and the like. They know that this will be extremely preliminary, but they also know they need to begin somewhere in the process of drafting a big opportunity statement that can soon be used to focus the meta-net's work.

They begin their first draft, aware that with each conversation, with each new inclusion in the soon-to-be-formed meta-net, the articulation of optimal outcomes will change. They know they are engaged in an iterative process that will continue. That is part of what makes it alluring, in a way. It is already enlivening them, putting into their hands, something that has the possibility of more positively impacting what the Security Council can bring to the Secretary-General and the General Assembly. Being part of "something we can all do together to pre-empt this threat to our global community" is tremendously exciting. Even if it doesn't stop or substantially curb existing cyberwarfare, they know it will impact it, and possibly turn the track of history toward a less contentious, more meta-humanity friendly direction.

This is what the team comes up with as a first draft of their big opportunity statement:

> "The Security Council could utilize the UN's unique convening power for the purpose of our collective future, to facilitate new dialogues between representatives of the global tech community, the Security Council and its relevant committees and staff and other appropriate UN representatives. These dialogues would make as a priority, the refinement of a change vision and development of innovative, viable strategic initiatives putting meta-humanity concerns at the forefront of cybersecurity in our increasingly borderless world.

> "Using this vantage point of meta-humanity concerns as a key part of the opportunity that lies

within the grasp of this group developing strategic cybersecurity initiatives, would newly enliven discussions in different ways than are typical Security Council, post-problem, cleanup-the-mess types of negotiations. This meta-humanity perspective would also inform discussions among those of the tech community in ways they could not have previously envisioned outside the halls of UN meeting rooms.

"Additionally, Member States, UN officials and staffers, engaged NGOs and eventually the larger public will better understand how these new lines of action can better address the currently out-of-control transnational criminal elements that are utilizing the latest technologies for their communication, money flow, organizing, recruiting, sourcing and implementation."

Step 3: Form the Meta-Net

Forming the meta-net is also an important part of the work. To more fully understand how to get a meta-net up and running, I refer you back to Kotter's book. It will not take you long to get through it and the concepts are easy to grasp. He is an esteemed academic, yet he presents his approach with a simplicity that may belie its efficacy.

Some points to remember about these teams per Kotter's approach:

1. Leadership (in this case the Member State initiating the formation of the meta-net) will naturally form its steering committee (guiding coalition in Kotter's plan) to facilitate the meta-net's work. This steering committee would be small and engaged throughout the meta-net's process.

2. Forming a volunteer corps for a particular meta-net is where things get exciting. The volunteers not only get to contribute their ideas, experience, knowledge and insights to the evolution of strategic initiatives, but also they get to connect their innovations and initiatives for change back to those leading their organization and arena of endeavor.

3. The opportunity to be on a meta-net is one of the natural ways that leadership is nurtured, and this further strengthens the organization as a whole. As for non-UN participants (such as expert members of a UN meta-net), their participation at the UN would widen and broaden their experience and expertise to include global issues perhaps not heretofore listed on their resumes. Techies would take note of this rather solid side benefit.

Scenario Sequence 3

The guiding coalition will have all but formed by this stage from the staff of Member State's Mission to the UN as a steering committee. This steering committee will oversee the outreach to potential volunteers and make the final choices from those who apply to join the meta-net.

Aware that the meta-net team will benefit from having diverse perspectives and skill sets to energize and stimulate thinking all around, they will also work to get geographically diverse applicants as well as volunteers from the relevant UN offices, known agencies and NGO alliances who specialize on the topic.

The guiding coalition will also by now, have reached back into their own nation's cybersecurity experts and through them and other civil society connections, seek out some of the world's best in their field. They will include both those who are, and who are not, engaged in governmentally managed cybersecurity issues. The intent will be to bring as full a range of actors into discussions as possible.

Remembering that the point of the meta-net is to engage those who are energized by the big-picture opportunities, invitations are one thing; however, the applications of those interested will then have to be filtered before final decisions are made as to who will join the meta-net team.

Applicants will be informed that their participation will be on their dime and on their time, so only the most interested will even apply. Finding a balance of participants will have to be kept in mind, aware that bringing the change vision and understanding of the strategic initiatives will be part of the work of the meta-net team. The volunteers will need to come from every level of the UN, from senior management to field offices, top tech entrepreneurs, developers and hackers, civil society associations and institutes and even tech media.

All applications and the chosen team will have a clear timeline for participation, and many will probably have to plan to be in New York for the month. The meta-net will be for those wishing to permanently impact how the Security Council will deal with cybersecurity issues in the future. It will require those folk being prepared to clear their agendas for most of the month, or at least making themselves very available if they have to leave the process for brief amounts of time.

Step 4: Evolve Strategic Initiatives

The time-constrained work of the meta-net will be established at the inception when it is being convened to form. In many of the issues addressed by the UN, bringing in stakeholders who are not part of the UN family of organizations will be a key component of the work, and

UN-related meta-net team members will need to be ready to engage with very different perspectives than their own.

Remember, there will be advantages to having outside partners in this critical work, and in the beginning, the meta-nets will need to go through a wrestling process. These teams will need to identify up front what might be barriers to their process, and these will need to be addressed by the relevant parties or built into the recommendations for action that the meta-nets produce.

Although a meta-net would convene with a time frame set before it, they need not be cobbled, rather energized by a tight parameter. Within that frame, the meta-nets will realize that their meetings need to produce usable content, not in some distant tomorrow that never arrives, but in the immediate today when effective strategies and solutions are badly needed.

Scenario Sequence 4

This part of the scenario cannot be mapped out quite so well, as this is where the magic happens, where all involved wrestle with first understanding how their unique synergies and creative juices can be best employed. Egos notwithstanding, as no one in such a meta-net will have much shyness about their intellectual acumen on the topic at hand, the team members will have to find ways to congeal under the larger umbrella of the task entrusted to them.

The meta-net is very likely to come up with two or three proposals for strategic initiatives. These would then be presented to the Security Council, the Secretary-General and reported to the General Assembly. Of course, it will be up to the Security Council to vote on following through on any of this, but already, new discussions, new engagement is underway, the effects of which will continue to ripple out.

Step 5: Institute Change, Dissolve as Needed

Clarifying the recommendations for change and delivering these to the relevant parties will mark the significant progress for which the meta-net is convened. Progress will be specific in terms of the recommendations for change. When meta-net members begin to see the changes they are helping to institute, they can then move on, taking the lessons learned, along with any upgraded skills, into their next arena of work.

Scenario Sequence 5

At this stage, the Security Council would discuss and possibly vote on the strategic initiatives proposed by the meta-net. If these were seen to counter cyber threats or contribute to significant security safeguards going forward,

the Security Council could draft a resolution that would
set any or all of them in motion and assign as work for
the relevant organs, UN agencies or Member States as
appropriate. Alternatively, they could draft a report and send
it to relevant UN agencies or departments. Or finally, they
could simply turn them into another of history's footnotes,
hopefully for good reason and not due to conflicts of interest
at the national level.

No matter what the final determination of the Security Council, the two communities would both have new insights, along with the skin-touch experience of working within a meta-net to transform cyber threats into possibilities. All this would now belong to the larger group of participants and would filter out to impact those with whom they continue to work.

Meta-Nets and the UN

While the above scenario specifically takes place within the purview of the Security Council, this is by no means the only institutional area within the UN that could make use of meta-nets. In fact, it was during the 25th Crime Commission in Vienna the key connections for this book dropped into place. The dots connected all around one missing piece.

The theme of this Commission included the prevention of terrorism—an ongoing challenge for the Member States and the UN. All the pieces were there. I was at the commission to assist an NGO with a unique capacity for defusing religious extremism, make new international connections. They have proven their work many times over in the field throughout nearly two decades of consistent effort. Their stories are quite incredible, but I will not be able to go into all that here. The point is they have specific knowledge, skills, and methodologies for turning religious leaders who advocate violence into educators of peace. Their work is barely short of miraculous, and is a model that needs scaling up in a world suffering from potent pockets of unconstrained religious extremism.

UNODC's Civil Society Team with whom we more regularly work gave its support. UNODC's Office for the Prevention of Terrorism provided a speaker for the side event our NGO initiated. Then, the Mission of Morocco to the UN ran with it. As noted, what became more apparent after the success of this side event was the lack of clear next steps.

The discussion was: "Defusing Religious Extremism: Building The Capacity Of Conservative Religious Communities As Key Partners In Counter-Terrorism Efforts." Each presenter added to the discussion their organization's efforts to deal with what Douglas Johnston, President of the International Center for Religion and Diplomacy (ICRD) has called over the years, "the ideas behind the guns."

The Ambassador of the Mission of Morocco to the UN introduced the Marrakesh Declaration that has Islamic nations taking steps toward the rights of religious minorities in predominantly Muslim majority communities; Mr. Ulrich Garms of UNODC's Terrorism Prevention Branch outlined the mechanisms and work of UNODC to coordinate across the UN and with the Member States, counter-terrorism efforts; and Johnston outlined the specific grassroots work the ICRD is doing that effectively defuses volatile and violent groups.

The potential that lies within these three organizations alone is remarkable. Each was interested in working with the other. Clearly, interest, need, and capacity all gathered there in the Vienna International Center. The potential of these three groups alone was palpable, and yet so little resulted from all this effort. Why?

Since we are talking about organizational interaction, what was missing was a specific piece of social machinery. It was like having a computer, a printer and all the software needed to make an office run, but there were no cables or Bluetooth and protocols connecting these different components together into one larger functioning unit.

The conclusion is that even when NGOs, today's social technology innovators, devise powerful new models, they still need access to those individuals who can establish policy and take their work to scale. The UN has to be able to filter out the best of many possibilities and give their attention to those. The Member States have to find ways to make such models applicable to their unique, sometimes highly volatile and complex political circumstances.

In other words, there remains the urgent and unique work of creating strategic initiatives (cables) that ensure all these pieces are networked and engaged. Activating a meta-net would have ensured that the strategic initiative described above could take those next steps.

What I saw missing at the UN in Vienna, as I now reflect and realize I've also seen at similar scenarios in New York and Geneva, is a way to put all these individually brilliant, but disparate pieces together into working strategies. The mechanisms needed to turn innovation into social adaptation is simply nowhere to be found.

No matter the fine words or intent to include through meaningful partnerships with civil society, there is a lack of organizational means to accomplish this. The UN made a great effort to get all the equipment in the office and believed its work done. In Vienna and on many other occasions as well, there is no lack of need or interest on the part of UN stakeholders; rather there is a lack of meaningful connection mechanisms.

The very organization that needs to be the most effective in the world remains hobbled by its inability to adapt to 21st-century realities where governments are not the sole provider of structures and services. Even machines today are learning, but the UN? It remains locked in the 20th-century where nations were primary and transnational options were nowhere to be found. With globalization, changes in these perspectives are now imperative.

The most direct and doable solution is to augment the UN's existing structure to help it stay in sync with the rest of the world. Choosing adaptations that facilitate flexibility, encourage voluntary measures and generate partnerships, that champion meta-humanity can break the gridlock of sovereignty while maintaining human rights and global security.[13]

CHAPTER FIVE
Social Technology: The Hidden Keys

Throughout this book, I have urged the UN to consider and implement action-oriented meta-nets, and for good reason. There are times and places where the slow, contemplative path is well advised, and there are times, such as what we face today, when strategic thought with the full intent toward action is the better prescription.

This final section is a cautionary tale about the price of inaction. It took several years of post mortem reflection and forensics of a sort, but that failure to act left me with clues that unearthed some quite revealing answers. Those answers provide us with keys to unlocking the UN, and thus, our future.

This tale began just before the turn of the millennium. It is a story of how a bold and timely idea caught the hearts and minds of hundreds of concerned individuals, most of who were engaged in various ways with the UN. However, when it finally reached the launch phase, the initiative, by then a charter needing only the signatures of its authors and supporters, was suddenly set aside, effectively killing it.

This strategic initiative was quietly shut down by some of the key figures of the same well intentioned, but non-adaptive, hierarchical international NGO that had started it. This NGO had until that point, successfully championed an idea to create *a forum for the world's religious leaders to convene and through this initiative, to support the peace and security work of the UN*. The forum's main purpose and task would have been to address the very pressing issues that both united and divided religions, from past, but more importantly, recent and still raw current events.

How could good and capable people so inspired to break new ground at international and inter-religious levels have acted so poorly, and so opposite to their own stated goals?

As I investigated the many pieces of the story I am about to tell, it became clear to me not only what was in place that impelled them to make such an unfortunate decision, but also what was missing that prevented them from considering anything else. The clues led me to insights that have been outlined in this book as transilient leadership.

With a growing awareness of the significant problems that are possible when organizations are unable to evolve and adapt appropriate to their social environment, I have further come to realize that the UN is on a similar track. This is the cautionary aspect of my telling this story, and why I sincerely urge you to consider the roles you may yet have to play.

When Social Adaptation Fails...

The story begins with a bold initiative in the late 1990s. Some intense five years later, it ended as a perplexing failure to launch, with immeasurable losses and betrayal. Like most betrayals, it did not take place with a public announcement; rather, it took place behind closed doors, with whispers and knowing nods. It was, however, as duplicitous and lethal as Judas' kiss. What follows is a brief synopsis of that story.

As this initiative first began to gather steam, the Speaker of the House of the Philippines, Jose de Venecia said, "This is an idea whose time has come." The idea grew from private discussions, to ad hoc, then local and national meetings and finally to international conferences.

Participants in these discussions ranged from academes and activists, current diplomats and former heads of state, concerned members of the private sector and of course religious leaders from every major and many minor traditions. Eventually, after years of convening, they were able to draft a formal charter calling for the formation of the Interreligious Peace Council (IPC).

The idea, while quite simple in concept, required great courage and personal sacrifice by people from some 54 nations. Finally in Seoul, Korea, in August of 2005, the charter was to be adopted at an international meeting.

The final draft of the charter outlined a forum for representatives of religions from national and regional councils to convene and discuss urgent issues with which religions and their adherents contend. Naturally, this would have included addressing violent religious extremism, but would have also engaged a wide range of discussions and initiatives as to how the world's religions impact, both positively and negatively, all aspects of human life and culture.

Have you heard of such a council? Have you seen a press conference where its spokespersons conveyed reasoned responses to violent attacks perpetrated by religiously motivated terrorists? Have you read any of their proceedings? Have you noticed any conferences bringing together representatives from faith traditions most in contention to wrestle with these difficult issues affecting their millions?

Your answer would have to be, "No," because none of the above happened. Tragically, the vote for adoption of the charter was removed from the conference program. The afternoon before the document was scheduled to be signed, a small cadre of directors of the NGO mentioned above, unilaterally decided they would not see through the formation of the Council.

Their reasoning was odd. They were concerned that once the council was formed, they would no longer have a central role to play and in essence, lose control of it.

These were the very ones that had helped take their founder's vision from an idea to becoming an internationally supported initiative. They had coordinated and managed significant efforts including regional and preparatory meetings, engendered copious communications, and successfully urged many to donate funds in support of all these efforts.

Even though I was in the midst of much of that which transpired up to the launching of this initiative, it has taken me years to unravel what motivated those individuals to quash it prior to its inception. What I eventually uncovered was a thoroughly unexpected culprit in the Peace Council's demise.

I sensed there was something underlying this gut wrenching reversal, but could not clearly see what it was at the time, much as how the quiet butler in the room often goes unnoticed. Only much later did I make the connection that while people were involved and their personal leadership capacities played a significant role, what was also crucial was their having access to and using appropriate adaptive social technologies to match the growing network of contacts, information and knowledge required to implement this social innovation.

The NGO's organizational structure, that is, the social technologies the NGO implicitly employed, ended up hobbling their evolving work. The organization was unable to learn and adapt to the new needs of the evolving work the realization of the bold idea required.

This NGO was facing a juncture in their own journey, from envisioning a bold initiative, to working out the nuts and bolts of how to give it life, to finally launching the IPC itself. This last step necessarily meant letting go of the helm and allowing others to share in steering things forward. At this point the IPC would no longer require careful management and oversight. Handing over and sharing its guidance going forward needed transilient leadership and appropriate mechanisms.

I surmised that those few NGO leaders holding the reins throughout most of the process had not quite seen the last part coming. They now had to squarely face the end of one phase and the beginning of another. Frankly, they lacked the personal capacity to overcome their Lizard-Brain survivalist reaction. In other words, without having transilient muscles equipping them for the changes ahead, they could not approach this new unknown with a sense of anticipation and excitement.

Instead, they could only feel that something was going to be taken from them, which was true, but what was also true was that they would have been able to fully participate in the next new phase, were they only ready to adapt and continue to adapt. They needed to be forward, not backward looking, leading change, not maintaining status quo.

These aspects of transilience are what they lacked, and so they caved in to a gut level reaction arising from their lizard brains, a gnawing, vague sense that nothing was going to be the same and that somehow they might not be able to survive the transition. Fear, plain and simple, drove their decision, (L1-survival), augmented by an antiquated internal NGO culture (L2-social), that then made it very difficult for them to make a coherent rational (L3-strategic) step forward.

The antiquated Limbic-social mode to which I just alluded was perhaps the more problematic aspect of their process. Every organization creates and builds upon its own internal culture. Such organizational cultures become problematic when they operate as an unseen hand within the glove. In the case of this NGO, their internal culture had been silently, relentlessly working to allow its own rigid hierarchical structure to continue to weigh itself down over many years.

These first two L-dimensions in play at the time were strongly ensconced in the few representatives who conspired in that backroom decision to override years of effort that had brought them to that crossroad. As the charter neared signing, the leaders of this NGO focused backward, and wanted to keep things the way they had been up to that point. In essence, they wanted to continue on, as managers of the initiative, not as leaders in the dynamic changes that charter would inevitably unleash.

Imagine Thomas Jefferson withdrawing the Declaration of Independence hours before it was to be signed because he had this gut level feeling that maybe the whole thing was a bit too risky after all. This L1-survival reaction probably did gnaw at him as he authored a document citing inadequacies of a powerful empire. Fortunately, he rose above that sensation and later enabled others to create a constitution ensuring a freer (L2-social) culture based upon innovative (L3-strategic) political structures.

Sadly, those NGO leaders did not rise above their instincts and failed to hand the charter over to the two-hundred-plus conference attendees waiting to take on their role. The participants' more than capable hands had anticipated this moment, and for many of them, the charter had begun to feel like a sacred trust. Those hands left that conference empty, with many an owner's mind perplexed, and their hearts saddened and confused as to why.

How miserable it is that this lofty effort to create a forum for the world's religious leaders to engage some of today's most troublesome issues came to such an inglorious smothered end. To this day, when I watch another report about a religiously motivated attack, I wonder, "What if?" What if that council had been launched?

I suspect that the Council would have gone through a rather chaotic growth process. On the one hand it may have devolved into an impossible mess, while on the other, the council just may just have found its way. The point is, we will never know. Hearts were broken at the time, and with delay after delay, eventually there was no way to regroup and start all over as it had taken years to arrive at that moment of birth.

As courageous humans do, those special people who volunteered in helping to author, support and seek to sign the charter, eventually moved on. The point here is not to bemoan all that effort, nor spend undue time blaming others. As a scientist, I do believe that in the end, no energy expended is ever truly lost. Hopefully what was misplaced there can help provide some light for others here, especially the point about transilient leadership in today's fast-paced, globalizing world.

The tale above indicates what happens when we are not entirely aware of, nor attendant to, all three dimensions of leadership. Transilient leaders work to ensure that organizational initiatives devised are also properly implemented. This means factoring in all three "L" drivers—survival, social and strategic—and not remaining content with redrawing the organizational chart.

We often focus on the strategic aspect of our efforts, especially when it comes to making significant changes. However, consider how often we meet in committees and form task forces that eventuate in little to no real change.

This is why I urge that we pay attention to our lizard-survival and limbic-social drivers when advocating for change, realizing that these drivers are in all of us, even those wanting and not just those resisting change. They both show up as personal motivation and as corporate culture.

As such, they comprise the uncharted and often overlooked side of each organization that is nevertheless constantly at work, even if unconsciously. In fact, they are more of a factor when operating unconsciously.

There are ways to address these undercurrents that emerge, sometimes in blatant fear mongering, ridicule and character assassination, but they can also be subtle tactics by which one or a few stall progress. The main point here is that without paying attention to all the drivers along with the more obvious strategic changes, we risk missing what is really happening when an initiative begins to dissipate with a self-imposed myopia that can be deadly.

The lessons I learned from my part in the above story have given me a keen eye when it comes to the pluses and minuses of any organization, no matter how small or large, how high its ideals, or how wide its scope of influence.

I could have furthered diagnosed what had transpired using the X, Y, Z axes of 3D leadership as well, but there is no need to belabor the analysis. However, having both a transilient and a 3D perspective on leadership helps us factor into our assessments of what to do, and what to avoid, in each step of a change process. This is because we can and do often overlook these otherwise hidden factors, much to our organization's detriment.

CHAPTER SIX
Where is the UN Headed?

With these lessons and the future of humanity in mind, it is not a big leap to wonder if the UN is currently on a track toward growing relevance or new levels of ineffectiveness.

I do not want, for a moment, to give short shrift to the enormous and often thankless task with which the UN has to contend. It has limited resources and yet must accept and respond to the implicit and unrealistic expectations placed upon those who work with and within it. The UN as a whole and the individuals that serve the organization, struggle heroically to maintain their funding, fulfill their mandates, and make efforts to effectively lead peace and development across 193 nations.

These are all the more reasons the UN needs the best and brightest, and most aptly motivated individuals to come through its doors, but more importantly, to use social technologies that could upgrade its organizational structure and keep it more vitally in the game.

Growing pressure for large-scale change at the UN has been underway for many a year, and quite frankly, began soon after its inception. My sense is that this pressure will continue to come to bear unless the UN can adapt internally by adopting well-placed and more agile mechanisms within the structure and culture that already exists.

In May of this year, when I participated in the 25th Crime Commission held in Vienna, I could not help but notice all the ways in which the sovereign, state-based machinery was in place and performing as usual. Resolutions were passed, themes discussed, new connections made, useful information shared, and significant progress was made on a number of issues that included resolutions on:

- Preventing and combating trafficking in human organs and trafficking in persons for the purpose of organ removal;
- Promoting legal aid, utilizing a network of legal aid providers;
- Restorative justice in criminal matters.
- Strengthening crime prevention in support of sustainable development, including sustainable tourism;
- Mainstreaming holistic approaches in youth crime prevention.

UNODC's clear processes and policies, roles and rules made this significant work possible, and the outcomes of the Crime Commission were consistent with the strategies outlined in E/RES/2012/12. Many commented that, compared with other Commissions, things moved forward very well at this Commission.

However, this version of progress, while significant and essential, is only half of what is needed. No organization, nor any government, no matter how powerful, is exempt from facing today's growing global turmoil and escalating threats.

If the various parts of the UN, the ones with the power to initiate change, still need to be convinced that business as usual is nothing other than a form of death by delay,[1] what lies ahead? I have some hope in that regard as I notice how seeds of innovation are already scattered throughout the UN system.

For example, as the representative of an organization that specializes in defusing violent religious extremism and as a chair of the Alliance of NGOs on Crime Prevention and Criminal Justice, I serve in various ways with the Civil Society Team of UNODC.

This team works with coalitions of civil society organizations to better address drugs, corruption and the prevention of terrorism. In fact, it was their efforts to support coalitions of civil society organizations that first triggered my connecting of the dots between Kotters' system and the UN, and then finally to the extraordinary usefulness of meta-nets.

However, it doesn't take long to see that the mechanisms for their work to connect with entities outside the UN system are close to non-existent. The UN is still a mature, insular hierarchical entity that has not significantly adapted its functioning, despite huge social changes, since 1945.

To convey this analogy on the personal level, I certainly appreciate the beauty and magnificence of the 1946 Cadillac, powered by an elegant Victory Engine, but it is no match for the self-driving Tesla S with the 'Ludicrous Speed' package that goes from 0 to 60 in 2.8 seconds.

So then, why do we continue to abide with 1945 social mechanisms that are simply not adequate to counter today's threats, such as non-state actors tapping top hackers to interfere with vital internet connections and major markets? How can it be possible for mid-20th century social technologies to keep up with the blizzard of global changes confronting us in this 21st century? The conclusion can only be that the imperative to adopt new social technologies to keep the UN competitive and relevant is urgent.

Another factor in this bifurcation of actual tech versus social tech adaptation began showing up in the late 1990s resulting in the suppression of social innovations by an "attitudinal governor" of sorts (correlates to mechanical governors that throttle an engine's power so as to modify input and that cannot be properly handled by all parts of the system). This meant lost opportunities for the UN, the supposed global leader of politico-social innovation.

By the late 1990s there was a surge in sheer numbers of nonprofits and NGOs worldwide, and many actively engaging the UN. This technically empowered capacity for international activism coupled with their newfound communications capacities that shone a light on many problematic situations simultaneously put many governments on the defensive.

Remember the 1999 Seattle WTO protests when NGOs became "the NGO swarm?" Yes, they flexed some muscle, but the consequent result came from a subtle chilling of relationships between many Member States and the technologically empowered civil society. That chill became clearer over time as NGOs and civil society members found accessing and/or engaging in UN meetings, even when allowed to attend, more and more difficult to do.

These changes were justified, as "We do not have the resources to handle the number of NGOs wanting to participate." Instead of that being an indicator for the need for adaptation, it became justification of limiting access, hence a social governor.

At the same time new, rising dot-com enterprises were becoming the poster children of Wall Street. Two different attitudes about innovators and their innovations were forming as one century closed and a new one opened.

Today we can see that tech start-ups made it out of the gates much faster and have gone much farther than their NGO social entrepreneur counterparts. But luckily, the story is not finished. After all, we are still writing it as we go along.

What if the UN and its Member States, as part of their re-invention for the larger meta-humanity social good, were to take on an equivalent role of those angel investors who helped make possible the vast array of amazing technologies we currently enjoy and often have far-reaching benefits for meta-humanity? Silicon Valley angel investors put in money, but perhaps equally importantly provide guidance and nurture to help neophyte start-ups move beyond their initial project focus to become strong and successful enterprises able to survive even in today's turbulent economic environment. Whole new businesses, including tech incubators, have grown up as an affirmation of the value of emerging technologies to society.

What if the UN and its Member States similarly nurtured promising NGOs and the larger contributing civil society, if not financially, at least with the kind of supportive access needed to better navigate and function effectively in intergovernmental environments? The win-win would be that the Member States would be able to benefit from the social innovations they nurtured in the NGOs.

Could the UN and civil society form generative partnerships that more expediently bring social innovations into play, countering and outsmarting terrorists and other criminal elements? What if the UN spearheaded the creation of a social ecosystem that nurtured social entrepreneurs and better prepared themselves to ramp-up implementation of promising practices?

Today's terrorists, criminal hackers and instigators of cyber warfare tactics are quite virile. They do not lack potency by any measure of that word. Can we afford to allow our United Nations, the one globally focused organizational vanguard, to lag further and further behind, to become, in contrast, impotent? No! We simply cannot.

One of Two Endings Coming Soon

There are two possible endings for this story of UN evolution. The first is where the UN continues with business as usual, steadily continuing its all but quaint practices, unfazed by the pace of change in our fast-moving society.

The second ending envisions the UN in a relentless pursuit to remain relevant by serving the public good more effectively in the midst of increasing complexity, adapting and utilizing emerging technologies and tapping the insights of those at the cutting edge. This ending could unfold in many extraordinary ways, starting by reframing the UN as adaptive, actively pursuing innovation, with the larger good of meta-humanity truly in mind.

By modeling transilient, transformational, organizational change, it would be showing existing organizations, be they governmental, service, or private sector, that the UN as a major social institution can innovate and step up to better meet the challenges of this century. In this way, the UN would be advocating for and leading change.

Furthermore, with the UN modeling proactive, innovative change from the inside out, it will then be better positioned to provide counsel on meaningful change as a viable alternative to violent revolution. My hope is that this book can help unlock the stalled conversations about UN renewal and start a new storyline of UN organizational innovation.

The tech tsunami is coming. Its impact depends in large part, on how quickly our social systems—our *social technologies*—adapt and innovate to ensure society as a whole can handle the sea change that is coming with artificial intelligence and increasingly autonomous cyber-physical systems.

Perhaps someone in an office, an agency or even a small nation steps up in the General Assembly or in ECOSOC, and having investigated this approach, decides to be bold, to test it out on one particular agenda item. Perhaps out of sheer desperation a few months down the line, someone else tries something akin to meta-nets at a time and a place where they see fit.

Perhaps their first foray brings amazing results. Perhaps the next try is not as successful. Who knows? At least change will be underway and naturally new things will be devised.

I remain excited about the possibilities that can emerge from new conversations and the exploration of different ways for UN stakeholders to engage one another. As I have already surmised, I believe the most potentially productive forays will be those made by the tech community if they are welcomed at the UN.

As big as the threats are from emerging technologies, there are even greater opportunities for human progress. It depends on how we want to proceed forward, with transilience or reluctance, anticipating change or resisting it.

We are in the drawdown phase of the tech tsunami, and there is yet time to act. There is time to create, respond, and take advantage of the challenges in front of us. Let us find ways, small and large to unshackle our loftiest and still critically needed global politico-social experiment—the United Nations.

Otherwise, we may yet one day find ourselves confronted with rice fields afire on top of a hill while mourning huge losses in a washed out village below.

Please join with others and me in the conversation about meta-nets and how we might unlock the United Nations. There are many opportunities already possible and many not yet devised. Visit or ping me any time:

www.StrategicSolutions.onl.

PART II
A Word to Major Stakeholders

About the Letters

Whether it is a roaming asteroid on a crash course with earth, the inevitable extinction of our aging sun, a benevolent god or fickle forces determining our future, it still makes sense for us to act as if the health of life on planet earth is up to us. We are left, therefore, to decide what it is that we will do to shape our future.

I was trained in the hard sciences, but also chose to soften its pragmatic grasp of the universe with philosophy and theology. I love how mathematics gives us ways to work with our phenomenal and amazing world. Words are less direct, but I love them as well for a different reason. They are magic.

When magic was the dominant way of comprehending the world, words conveyed power and meaning. Moreover, they still do today, even if the how is understood differently.

Our words do matter: the words we use to envision and talk about our world, the tone of our constant inner self-talk; the depth of our daily external conversations with others; all these create the world within which we live and act. Words, in this way, are indeed powerful. Our iterative choice of words sustains and sometimes newly defines our world and our actions in it. Consider the impact of bullying. Even if there isn't any physical violence, the recipient is nonetheless profoundly impacted, bruised in places that cannot be seen but are nonetheless very real.

Our choices arise from the differences we notice—or don't—and are shaped by the words we choose to give voice to each of those differences. We are all molding our world each day in this way, through the magic of words.

Therefore I write these letters to you in the hope that words can once again do a little magic—catch your interest, move your heart, or perhaps inspire a new thought or action. Why should I write to you in the format of a personal letter? Because you are a stakeholder in my future as I am in yours, and I am hoping that we might look again at where we are going together and when needed, adjust our course.

Perhaps the UN will become newly energized, finding ways to be a stronger springboard for strategic action. Even better, I hope for a UN that attaches some part of itself to the social equivalent of a SpaceX Falcon 9 so it will go boldly "where no-one has gone before."

As I reach to find the right words for each of these letters, my heart says a short prayer: "For us all."

Letter to the Member States

Your Excellency:

It may now be quite some years since you began your journey as an ambassador representing your country to the United Nations. How did you come to this task? Did you aspire to a diplomatic role to contribute to international affairs on behalf of your nation or did you somehow accidentally fall into this complex world of politics, policy, and protocol?

While politics and I have not always seen eye to eye, life found a way to bring me to UNHQ in New York in 1997. Since then I have come to see the UN in many ways, including as a petri dish—a rather remarkable way to encounter some of the greatest and the worst of humanity. I believe it is this international space that can incubate some of the boldest, meta-humanity leadership.

I realize you are also well aware of the pace of threats in an increasingly tech-leveraged world and how they threaten even the largest of traditional companies and organizations. The challenges of transnational crime and terrorism are perhaps the most obvious.

These problems so easily obscure both the UN's efforts to "save succeeding generations from the scourge of war..." and the Charter's call to "promote social progress and better standards of life in larger freedom." I urge you nevertheless to consider these threats as cloaked strategic mega-opportunities.

Claiming the possibility of there being significant opportunities for humanity behind the complex threats and challenges our world faces today may be a bold statement. But I contend that challenging times require bold leadership and atypical action, not business as usual.

I also wish to suggest a framework for action that is completely doable, and when championed by the Member States of the United Nations, will open up unprecedented standards of life in larger freedom.

My faith lies in the extraordinary minds, hearts, and souls of many I have met, come to know and had the honor to work with over the years at the United Nations.

This transilient framework calls for the formation of small networks of stakeholders (meta-nets) to work with various Councils, committees or agencies when significant threats challenge the existing structure's capacity to respond adequately.

This may sound far-fetched or simply too little too late, but how many years of travel were already under humanity's belt before the simple little compass came along to revolutionize navigation? Today we have a GPS in our pockets – how magical is that?

Small pivotal changes can make a world of difference, and I urge you to read up on meta-nets and to envision what they can do beyond the ideas presented in this book. For their real strength is in how they come together, their mandate, the members on the teams, how they operate and who convenes them.

Excellency, in addition to all your current state-divined mandates, Member States are in the unique position to dramatically change today's critical conversations about who we are as humanity, as meta-humanity.

I urge you to take the lead. The United Nations is your theater of action, and it is best positioned to convene, formulate and capitalize on global-level strategic challenges by aligning around meta-opportunities.

If you do not, who will enable and lead the UN to step up to new levels of relevance, engagement, and leadership?

I would be happy to answer any questions you may have.

I remain,
Your Excellency,
Sincerely yours,

Karen Judd Smith
www.StrategicSolutions.onl

Letter to the Secretary-General

Mr. Secretary-General:

First of all, Mr. Secretary-General, congratulations.

So few leaders would make it through ten years as head of UNHCR with the heart for more of the kind of work that yet needs to be done. You must have a profound faith in humanity along with a burning desire to act, because your colleagues have now entrusted you to take the helm to move the United Nations forward in a century fraught with unprecedented upheaval and uncertainty.

Please allow me to make three simple appeals that sum up as one recommendation: Lead. Lead. Lead. You have the position and with it comes the great opportunity to unlock the potential within the United Nations and the peoples it serves. You have formidably capable Under-Secretaries-General and staff to fulfill the management needs. However, you alone can give voice from the top of the UN mountain to "We the peoples of the United Nations…" in all the villages below.

Yours is the voice of our meta-humanity, of who we are at our best. Please remind us, often, of who we can be, not only who we have been. Remind us of what we have done well, and that we have all that we need to accomplish what yet lay ahead. Be that voice that speaks to our heads, our hearts and our souls as the human race, especially when the loudest voices are clamoring for far short of that best.

Then, to enable us to act better as humanity, an updated UN is urgently needed as we face increasingly complex threats leveraged by technological advances. Just as transnational criminals and terrorists are agile, enhancing their capacity to act and achieve their goals with the latest technologies, so too the UN needs to adopt new strategies and mechanisms to engage the best hearts, minds and technologies to replace its current last-century thinking, structures and stop-gap measures.

For this reason, I recommend a simple yet revolutionary social technology as an internal, organizational upgrade. Just as downloading a GPS app onto our mobile devices can turn even the most directionally impaired person into a keen navigator (my husband, for example), so too can meta-nets propel the UN toward its overall goal of making the world a safer and better place for all humanity.

One key meta-net I envision that can unlock the leadership of the UN involves engaging the relatively young leaders and entrepreneurs of the technology sector. In their hands lies a vast array of innovative thinking and doing that is capable of infusing the UN with new ways to respond to this century's challenges.

The tech community is far-flung, and though they speak many languages, they also converse in one tongue: technology. As such, they provide a networking capacity heretofore not experienced by even the best diplomats of the UN's Member States. If the UN can embrace them as real partners, they will, in turn, come to realize what it means to be a global citizen.

The UN not only has much to receive from the tech community, but it also has much to offer them: a global arena that naturally elevates their point of view from the tech village level to the UN mountain top of humanity writ large.

It is into your and your staff's capable hands, that I place my hope that such can happen, and this book, as a kind of map to chart ways forward.

As a global citizen and representative of civil society at the UN, I will also continue to lend appropriate and respectful assistance toward accomplishing the recommendations of this letter.

I remain,
Your Excellency,
Sincerely yours,

Karen Judd Smith
www.strategicsolutions.onl

Letter to Secretariat Staff

Dear Colleague:

I have met many of you over the last almost twenty years, and I have always been astonished at how deep your desire is to help our world become a better place. In you, I have seen the irrepressible spirit of hope and a heart for humanity, though I recognize it is not easy to maintain such generous good will.

I too believe there are extraordinary possibilities that the UN can uniquely help realize. I also believe that in today's fast-changing world we need to upgrade our organizations to better suit this increasingly turbulent new world.

Agility and adaptability are currently missing from the UN's descriptors, but could easily be added in. Just as a smartphone is personalized for particular uses by adding in new apps, so too can the UN become more relevant by taking on specific tasks that are urgently needed with the aid of some key social apps.

In other words, organizational innovation isn't as hard as it sounds, and the UN does not require charter change or Security Council restructuring to unlock the potency of each one of you, what you know, and what could be done better.

My intent in writing this book is simple: to introduce for discussion and consideration a social technology or social app that can unlock the UN. I urge you to think about how these social technologies called meta-nets could easily be implemented to help devise strategic initiatives where needed—for your office, your agency or your organization.

Sometimes solutions are much easier than the complex problems with which we currently wrestle. How simple is it to put in a destination and push the "Go" button on your mobile device these days? Who would have thought navigating your way across a city you have never visited could be so simple?

The UN is a unique and extraordinary organization with many of the world's very best team members—what more could we want? It is simply this: to tap even more of the very best from our global community, let these meta-nets unleash new energies and direction so we can leap forward, rather than remain constrained by past dictates. And yes, make the world a better place.

Please do not hesitate to contact my office with any questions you may have.

I remain,
Sincerely yours,

Karen Judd Smith
www.strategicsolutions.onl

Letter to NGO Representatives

Dear Colleague:

Working with you and the diplomatic community on this UN mountaintop for the last twenty years has been an honor. In my youth, I climbed to the peak of Mount Semeru (Mahameru) in Java, Indonesia. That journey provided unexpected life-changing experiences that widened and matured my perspectives

The view of humanity from the UN vantage point changed me perhaps in similar ways to the experience of astronauts seeing the earth from space where the only real borders are those between land and sea, high and low air pressure in the atmosphere, and then the planetary and extra-planetary boundary.

I began to look for ways that our social systems and processes, as well as our words and deeds, could both acknowledge and value difference (boundaries) and yet be radically inclusive (one planet).

During this journey, I have also sought to find ways NGOs and the larger civil society can more effectively bring our innovations to the ongoing work of making our world a better, safer, friendlier and more magnificent place for all, "in greater freedom." To this end, I hope you will find in this book, a map of sorts for you and your NGO in these pivotal times.

You may notice that in chapter five we have drawn parallels between the evolution of NGOs as social entrepreneurs and innovators and tech start-ups as tech entrepreneurs and innovators. Sadly, NGOs had to battle forward under a less than favorable public hue and cry since the late 1990s when NGO activists were depicted as "the NGO swarm."

At that time, many a diplomat listened with their survivalist ear rather than their strategic mind. The distancing of Member States from NGOs has questionably changed since them, no matter the appearance words may imply. Meanwhile, tech start-ups were the sought-after poster children of Wall Street and given every advantage from the private sector, the more prominent of which were named as angel investors.

The main point of this story and this book is simple: the future of humanity lies with both the evolution of technology and the largely overlooked social innovations, these latter being the realm of expertise of NGOs and other civil society actors.

Because the physicality of technology naturally exudes must-have sexiness, and tech's critical social innovation counterpart does not, it is overlooked by many. It is not that difficult to agree that much of today's turmoil arises from an imbalance between tech innovation and social resistance to change. Technology surges forward while our social organizations and institutions struggle to adapt and remain relevant in a decentralizing, increasingly open-sourced world.

Still, no matter the good or the bad of why we are where we are, I urge you as a social entrepreneur and innovator, to continue to lean into your work, for social innovations are needed all the more today. They need to be better understood, better valued, adopted and scaled.

I can only hope that as the UN and its Member States rise to meet today's challenges, they will do so through agile, focused partnerships with NGOs and larger civil society.

Therefore, as those individuals who understand how to work in the landscape of Member States and international organizations, I hope you can stretch yet again to help others who have never worked within the UN system, to better find their way through the often confusing intergovernmental woods.

Please consider building into your network and organization, places to connect with the tech community. There are many fine young men and women ready to link their daily work to the larger social good. These individuals need meaningful bridges to the still arcane global work of the UN and efforts such as these can be mutually beneficial.

As we continue our efforts, I can only hope that meanwhile, the UN family of organizations can see the urgent need to adapt and so will soon seek full-bodied partnerships when and where needed.

To our future, in larger freedom,

Sincerely,
Karen Judd Smith
www.StrategicSolutions.onl

Letter to the Tech Community

Hi:

How would you handle this scenario?

At 5:17 P.M. today you receive a note from a colleague saying she discovered that someone else in their software is using one of your carefully crafted signature algorithms or source code. The note also mentions that your code in this new software environment seems to have created vulnerabilities that you have no chance to address. What is more, these vulnerabilities are putting lives at risk.

The scenario continues. Tomorrow morning you will receive an invitation to work in New York with an expert team on a counter to that software that would protect those lives it currently puts at risk. If you choose to join this team, there will also be an additional opportunity to think at a larger level, with people who work on global security issues, international law, human rights and so on, to envision what behind these threats are the big opportunities that they currently cloak.

This invitation is not for a new job or position—there isn't even any pay involved—but an opportunity to collaborate with a diverse, world-class team of tech, policy, and politicos as a volunteer.

This work would be more than a catching and patching of bad code. This team would help shape strategic security initiatives at the UN by focusing more on the opportunities that lie beyond threat and reaction to those threats. Your practical knowledge of cybersecurity and big-opportunity thinking along with your capacity to continually integrate diverse factors and user needs are why you would participate.

All this, in a nutshell, is the "why you, why now" to join a strategic partnership team or meta-net with some unity of the United Nations. Technology is impacting and improving life the planet over. Its very presence is also creating new vulnerabilities that our social systems are not yet capable of handling. There is also good reason to believe that the human resources, perspectives, and practices specifically available in your community can help form unique partnerships capable of unlocking what the UN is: "We the peoples of the United Nations."

Already, you are redefining security and technical possibility with every keystroke that drives the information, automation, and access revolution forward. While what you do is often vital to us all, for your future and sake, I urge you to extend yourself and bridge to other areas of life that cannot be experienced in codes and programs.

Whether or not you envision yourself as a global citizen, information technologies are today's ground zeros of many a battle between efforts to protect society and at the same time ensure individual freedoms. It matters what you do both as a techie and as a citizen of planet earth.

While I do not have the authority to invite you to join a meta-net associated with the Security Council, I can invite you to join a nascent network of technology experts and their organizations interested in ways that technology can contribute to peace and security. This network functions in conjunction with the Alliance of NGOs on Crime Prevention and Criminal Justice, a wide-ranging group of international non-governmental organizations working with the UN Office on Drugs and Crime (UNODC).

If you have comments or questions, ping me @karenjuddsmith or www.StrategicSolutions.onl

Karen Judd Smith

Appendix & Resources

Appendix A:
The Solutions Matrix™

.

To speak of transilient leadership is to focus on leadership
with an emphasis on constructivism. It is a way of thinking
that relies upon a positive, forward-looking point of view,
rather than a backward, mulling over the past point of view.
For those making an effort to increase their capacity to exercise
their transilient muscles then, here are a few rules of thumb
that will help set you up for success.

Transilient Rules of Thumb

- **You are accountable for solutions, not responsible
  for problems.**

The transilient leader emphasizes accountability for
solutions and is not overly concerned about who to blame
and thus, shame. When pursuing positive change through
the construction of solutions, blame and shame tactics are

not only futile but also, they directly diminish our capacity to interactively construct solutions by wasting our most important resources — time and energy.

Drilling down on problems to find out who was at fault, what they did, and when they did it, only gives everyone more information about the problem, but it does not provide any information toward a real solution. Of course, if someone performed in an unethical or immoral way, then yes, that has to be addressed. But even there, the focus is not to dwell on that process, instead to quickly move on from the lesson learned and put one's efforts into discovering solutions.

Blaming and shaming are soul sucking enterprises that embroil us in back and forth, offense and defense, name-calling and backstabbing, alliance-building and ego-salvaging efforts. Transilient leaders don't engage in these downward spiraling tactics. They understand that transilience is the capacity to get from one place to the next, and the next place they want to arrive is where an effective solution can be implemented.

- Look for what is going right and do more of that.

Transilient leaders are always looking for what is going right, and finding ways to encourage themselves and others to do more of that, or something very similar to that. In the doing of such, unexpected side effects occur, a major one being the unexpected happiness factor! After all, isn't it freeing to be looking for solutions rather than wallowing in the depths of problems? Sure, problems are everywhere, and we can certainly focus all our attention on them, but what would you rather be doing? For those focused on finding and constructing solutions, all that wallowing is just, well, muddy.

- We already have what we need to construct solutions.

Another thing to notice when engaging a transilient leadership mode is that we can use prior successes to inform us as to what might work well going forward. When we add those past behaviors into our current situation, we at least begin with some confidence that our strategy will work because it has already worked before. Sometimes we have to tweak these applications to fit the new solution. Sometimes it will work even better than before and sometimes it will not work as well.

Transilience implies exploration that leads to innovation. We never quite know the outcomes of any action until we try them and then objectively take in the feedback that comes in the aftermath. We acknowledge the usefulness of any and all feedback, even negative comments. It's all information with which to create new solutions, going forward.

Transilience assumes that each of us is resourceful and has what we need to solve our problems, especially when we are prepared to construct solutions interactively with others. In this way, the capacity for and the potency of change, starting from within us and emerging outwardly in larger contexts that are appropriate for the solution(s) sought, is underscored. We each have the capacity to do something, not nothing. Finding the most effective way to do something is the key.

- Timely Evolution Versus Violent Revolution

This perhaps speaks more to the international level issues or very severe problems. It is worthwhile to mention, however, that the big things happening at the global level often correlate with smaller issues happening closer to home. The key here is to utilize urgency as your springboard for action. To ignore urgency and allow problems to devolve into crises happens all too often. It is called procrastination or death by delay, and all humans do it, some more and others less, but all of us tend to want to put off difficult decisions and actions for the next day (and the next).

There usually are alternatives to violent revolution and upheaval, but often efforts to implement change are not taken before that window of opportunity closes. It is possible for a change to iterate peacefully. Violent events and revolutions tend to take place when the longing for change becomes unstoppable, yet no systemic change takes place. Resentments arise in waves of violent action because no sufficient organizational-level intervention takes place in time. One voice is never enough.

In the months and years leading up to violence, the social tensions build from urgent to critical, much like the sheering forces in our tectonic plates when they are not relieved through smaller, forward-moving shifts. The result seen in devastating earthquakes and tsunamis can be compared to the devastation caused by civil war when pent up frustrations are unleashed in acts of terrorism and war.

Social circumstances do reach thresholds where the underlying tensions are too great. However, before these crises erupt, there is usually an urgency phase, when there is time to act energetically. Human society is far more pliable with many more pivot points for action than the earth's tectonic plates. Just as with tectonic shifts, warning signs are discernable ahead of time, and yet, even when detected, the seething unrest can be ignored or, effectively so, when those in positions of institutional power do not know how to address the tensions competently.

In fact, I believe that many of the major turning points in history marked by violent change were not conclusively inevitable at all stages but became so because those individuals or groups involved, inadvertently, or blatantly refused to initiate timely alternatives. Could they have?

In the bigger picture, our human learning curve may almost inevitably have to have included violence. The odds seem to have made it so thus far. But, I suspect and contend that it is a matter of the odds rather than inevitability. Perhaps a fine line in the end, but still, there is an important difference, especially in light of transilient leadership. Proactive, solutions focused, transilient leaders embrace difficult issues, finding within them the clues they need to create effective strategies to ameliorate or even entirely resolve those issues. And this work is not done alone. It utilizes our social nature and the resources of well-constructed organized systems.

As you can surmise from the above, the benefits of transilient leadership are multiple. Here then is a short list of some of those benefits. Transilient leadership:

- Makes difficult change possible and doable;
- Produces measurable results faster than most people think possible;
- Better utilizes the galvanizing power of the Meta-Humanity Effect
- Shifts individuals and groups from narrowing into reactive reductionism to engaging broader scopes of co-construction

The Solutions Matrix – Using Five Effective Questions (The 5Qs)

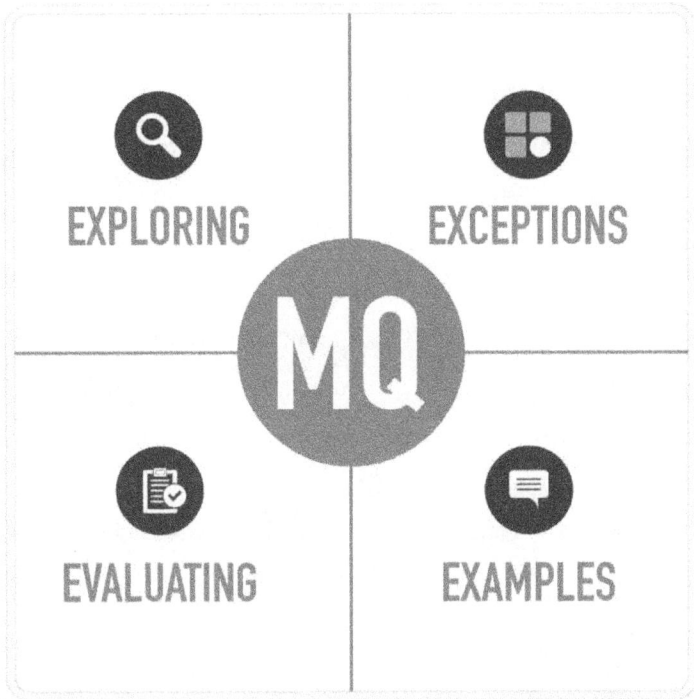

EXPLORING

EXCEPTIONS

MQ

EVALUATING

EXAMPLES

When addressing problems in a way that leads toward solutions, one of the first things that need to change is our language. Simply put, in the context of any problem, it is very useful to shift from problem talk to solutions talk. In this section, I provide a brief synopsis of a process called solutions focusing. This process has become generalized for use in personal development and corporate change and is derived from a clinical application under the genre of "Solutions Focused Brief Therapy."

I've included references to a few books that give an excellent overview of this topic if you want to delve further, but for our purpose here, I've honed what you need to know from my version of solutions focusing, into a handy guidance tool called, "The Solutions Matrix™."

There are five questions in the Matrix that work like a compass or GPS system to help you find your way through the thick, often disorienting bramble-ridden forest in which problems often entangle you. Problems tend to develop thorny branches that flourish with each complaint holding you ever more firmly in place. And of course, when something is problematic, you feel threatened and anxious, if not desperate, to get out of the woods altogether.

These five questions, while simple, lead us through a series of steps that keep us focused on clarifying a destination and constructing solutions that get us through and out of the woods. Because it makes use of the native difference engine built into humans, even using this system a little bit can bring about improvements immediately.

At the end of the chapter, I will walk you through a two-minute experiment that shows you how to use these five questions (5Qs) in real time. Let me be clear. I don't provide solutions. You will, with assistance from the 5Qs. This system helps you bring together some of the overlooked parts of your previous experiences, and the knowledge, and wisdom you've gleaned from them. It helps you discover the particular differences unique to you that can be used in specific instances to make even bigger differences that are possible when you recognize and then leverage them.

Four of the five questions make up the north, south, east and west points of the solutions compass that constitutes the Solutions Matrix™. These four questions center around one central question, and just like a compass, these questions are to be used as you move along the trail. Use them every few steps when you are struggling to find your heading, or as needed when you become more confident about where you are going.

The central question of the 5Qs is linked to the particular problem being addressed. Just remember, even a compass is of little use when all you know about your destination is that it is "not here." You have to devise a specific destination, even if only as a temporary placeholder. So, for each problem, this central question remains the pivot point for your solutions construction. What this first question does is help you clarify your destination, and asking it periodically helps you further hone where it is you'd rather be, per your solution.

What we are looking for here is a quantum leap of sorts, from problem articulation to solution description. This leap across a synaptic gap, from problem to solution is an essential step. This is the transilient component that when left out, keeps us entangled in problems and prevents us from constructing solutions.

Of course, all good leaders engage in the essential work of clarifying goals. However, an important caveat about creating goals that can be met is to ensure they are not a rearrangement of a negative problem-oriented statements and do evolve into descriptions for which actual steps can be made.

While this may sound simple in principle, in practice, developing a clear, desirable well-defined solution is rarely so. There is a certain stickiness to problems. We get used to them, even resign ourselves to them. The emotional toil of rising above our problems can at times seem daunting. Problems are messy and many are horrific when they involve a larger scope of humanity. Nonetheless, problems also point out where an underlying opportunity lies. The key to good solutions focusing practices is turning over those problem rocks and discovering the opportunity for solutions underneath.

Truly good solutions to seemingly intransigent problems don't necessarily have to have anything to do with the problem itself. Surprisingly, this is especially true when the issue has deep emotional context with historical and cultural underpinnings or other complicating factors.

Why? Because when a problem is so pervasive, doing anything different will lead to some solution. Think about a war in general. There is a build up of tensions, rhetoric, and arms. Finally, lines are crossed, and the conflict begins. It rages on, and after battles are won and lost, the tides turn, one way or another. Eventually, something different is tried—a white flag goes up and people sit down to discuss what else they can do, short of annihilating each other.

Awful problems then give us all the more reason to leave them behind and quickly get to work on articulating clear definitions of a solution. Again, though it seems ironic, every problem implies a solution. The fact that we recognize a problem already means we understand it for what it is: an obstacle to what we want. Now, we either begin to make steps toward what we want, but haven't clarified as such, or the problem is really not a problem—it may just be a fact of life.

Let's now take a brief look at the 5Qs and how to use them in the context of the Solutions Matrix.

Q1: The Miracle question

"Suppose that one night..."

The first step in creating a difference that will make a difference is to clarify what it is that we want as opposed to continuing to describe the problem that we don't want. This clarification is an ongoing process, not a one-time Q and A session that leads us to a one-time mountain top enlightenment.

It involves asking one strategic question that then allows you to imagine what you would be doing without having that problem at the center of your every waking hour (and many a restless night). In Solutions Focused Brief Therapy, this question is called, "The Miracle Question," because it asks us to consider the following:

"Suppose that one night while you were sleeping, there was a miracle... not just any miracle, but one that makes the problems you still wrestle with go away... just like that!

Since you were asleep and you didn't know the miracle happened, how would you know it happened? How do you discover things are now different? How will your colleagues know, without your saying a word to them, that things are different?"

The Miracle Question is intended to help us shift our thinking toward a clearer, more tangible envisioning of our solution—that also happens to be something we want. Remember the caveat, that there will always be more than one solution to every problem, so you don't have to fret or waste time devising the perfect solution. There isn't such a thing!

What I mean by this is that you concentrate on what the solution produces, not why it's a good solution. Get started heading toward your solution, and then you can tweak along the way.

Before you go onto the next four questions—just as a thought experiment—sit for a moment with this pivotal question. Think of some minor problematic thing going on in your part of the world, at the UN, or in your office or agency, or perhaps just the other day with a colleague in your tech start-up company. Close your eyes and visually walk yourself through a day without that "thing" happening. What do you notice about yourself as you first wake up? How do you feel without that problem hanging over you? How do you go about your first hour at work? How do you engage your colleagues?

Do this exercise from the standpoint of the problem no longer existing. Become a fly on your wall and watch yourself waltz through the morning without the weight of your problem clouding your thoughts or draining your energy If anything, this exercise allows you some freedom to imagine your life without that problem and see what it might be like otherwise.

Note how removing that problem, even if only in your imagination, how much lighter and clearer your thinking naturally becomes? Keeping problems reverberating in our minds darken and dampen our thoughts, restricting our capacity to envision life without them.

Hint: When you think of and act out of a sense of being free from a problem, bits and pieces of the solution naturally start forming in that problem-free space that opens in the absence of the problem. See how simple it is to create a difference that makes a difference!

One Final Note: The Miracle Question is a situation-specific version of this question: "Who am I and what do I really want?"

What do I mean by this? Each action we take is an act of self-definition. Each action defines whom we are choosing to be at that moment. We do this as individuals, as implicit or explicit members of groups or teams, of race, culture or nation. Sometimes, therefore, it is a valuable personal navigational tool that adds another line of direction to our self-understanding. We always need to know as accurately as possible: where we are now and where we wish to go. That way we can set a course. Otherwise, we flounder, and remain confused.

Using this aspect of our actions to help us get a fix on where we are and what we want, and helps us see more clearly the difference between where we are and where we want to be, especially when considering actions that will impact ourselves or others. By asking ourselves questions such as, "Is this truly who I am? Who do I want to be? Who am I? Is this what I really want for others and myself?" we may be surprised at the push that naturally comes in a direction toward our solution!

Let's proceed to the four remaining questions and the two-minute experiment where you can take these 5Qs for a short test drive.

Q2: Exceptions

When did things go right?

This question helps us focus on what is otherwise happening when the complaint is not. It helps us turn our quest for "not XYZ" into something specific, and importantly, something with which you have already had experience. You know what "it" (the exception to the problem) looked like, felt like and sounded like, but you likely haven't given it much thought.

There are often many more of these moments on planet earth than we at first think. After all, our world is not perfect which means no problem is perfect either. Further, we all have some proof of this because, at some point in our lives when problems did arise, there were times when it did not pervade and dictate everything and everyone around it.

Somewhere, there are exceptions to the problem and we just need to recall these moments in our experience. These exceptions are what we are looking for: specific times when the problem or complaint was not happening.

The simple question we then ask ourselves, to draw our attention to the empty room in which the elephant was not occupying the middle, is: "When did things go right?"

Another way of looking at this is that it does indeed help to remind us that not everything went wrong in any given situation. For example, in the aftermath of war, we look back and see that many despicable things happened, but that at the same time, heroic and humanitarian actions also took place.

The Miracle Question allows us to envision a future without the problem in it. Additionally, it frees our imagination to go wherever it wants into that imaginary future. The Exceptions Question encourages us to look back and see, no matter how brief, moments when the problem was not happening. This reassures us that such moments can happen again, to be sustained for even longer periods of time.

When we let ourselves realize that even in the worst of times, some right things occurred, we further loosen the grip that any particular problem may have over us. Realizing we do things well even in the midst of horrible situations is no small thing, and it is why this question is part of the overall Solutions Matrix.

Q3: Examples

How did I do that?

When we look back and recognize times that the problem was not afflicting us, we can then ask the next question: "How did I do that?" As you can see, nothing in this method is complicated; rather it is a gentle way to follow a particular path that will get you and your team where you want to go.

In other words, we are looking into those exceptions for specific examples of what we were doing other than wallowing in the problem (sorry, but that's what we humans tend to do). There will have been times when we were energized around something other than the problem. There are always times we can discover when we managed to do fairly well, sometimes even quite spectacularly!

Spending a bit of time reflecting on those actions, the ones that previously worked for us then helps us focus on what might work again—and if it does, to do so more consistently. All this moves us closer and closer to our solution where again, the problem is not happening.

These exceptions then become confidence builders and promising practice blueprints. They are confidence builders because you know that you can work these strategies again, albeit tweaked for the present context. They create a basis for blueprints. Whatever you did that worked in the past, can be adapted to your present situation as well. When you start from something that you know works, using that as your basic blueprint, it is much easier to create meaningful solutions.

In other words, problems reveal our weaknesses. When we dwell on problems, we tend to dwell on what we cannot do, and this fans the flames of hopelessness. It's so much easier to buckle under the supposed weight of the problem when viewed with a problem lens. On the other hand, when we look back and acknowledge one or two, or more, positive actions that we completed, we begin to realize our strengths.

No matter how small our achievements, they are nevertheless undeniable. So while these examples might seem to be little things, as we redeploy them in our present encounters, we can quickly find ourselves effecting real change, and in so doing, feel new inspiration for our daily endeavors.

Q4: Evaluation

What's different?

This question is all about measuring differences, and the simplest way to do this is through the use of scaling. This question helps us evaluate what we did at certain times and enables us to measure the difference made. We use a simple scale from 1-10, where we reflect on a particular day or experience and measure it against similar days or experiences. The scale is a continuum where "1" is a bad a day or experience and "10" is an optimal day or experience.

I teach this Matrix as a Life Coach, and I had one client who felt her life was so problem filled that she could not even relate to it using positive numbers. Instead, she scaled her days from "-10" to "zero," the latter for when at least nothing horrible happened. One day she called and said that the scaling had helped her focus on days when nothing terrible happened to the extent that she had begun to notice when a few good things did happen. She was pleased to share that she had changed her scale from a -5 to a 5+ to reflect the difference. Not much later, she adopted the 1 to 10 scale.

Noticing the difference through the scaling process is one way to sustain solutions construction and avert sliding back into a focus on problems. Scaling helps us keep our eye on the differences that make a difference—and keep us going in the direction we want. It's a visual and easily understood way of navigating our way toward successful solutions.

Each time we notice an up or down tick in the scale, our difference engine kicks in. Difference perceived as either good or bad, by the way, is just feedback. Scaling is not judgment, so it does not mean we are failing if we are working toward a solution and still have a low number day or did something that took us a notch or two lower.

It does indicate that it could be good to ask one or more of the 5Qs again, so you alter your course a bit, by doing more of what works and less of what does not. It is amazing how often we get stuck, and re-stuck in the same old ruts. Our focus on solutions slips, we start analyzing problems, and before we know it, we're back in that mind numbing, heart draining world of complaint again.

Once we embrace the scale as nothing more than honest feedback, we can have fun with it. Some days will challenge us. Some days will affirm us. Either way, we have a better idea of how we're doing, per our solutions, and this helps us hone even more efficient solutions, which then boosts our confidence and provides a positive feedback on the scale, which then energizes us to keep on going, expanding those solutions to work on bigger and tougher problems.

Q5: Exploring

What else? What is better?

I have gone skydiving numerous times, along with deep sea diving, riding a motorcycle up and down the east coast of Australia, backpacking solo through Southeast Asia, and earning a captain's license through the U.S. Coast Guard. I was for many years out on the ocean in both a public teaching and commercial fishing capacity. I've had my share of sailing adventures. In other words, I love exploring! But exploring is not only for Australians that have an incorrigibly curious mind and a penchant for a little danger.

The essence of this two-fold question is to push the envelope a bit and wonder what else is out there, and what might be even better than any solutions currently underway. This question urges you to explore, to reach for insights from your experiences. It encourages you to turn feedback into ideas for new strategies going forward. That is, no matter the kind of feedback, be it from the experience itself or from others involved, and whether pleasant or unpleasant, get ready to accept it without defense so you can then explore ways to make it meaningful for you. That is how you use each experience, good or bad, to your advantage. That is how you make your life work for you. Even negative comments can lead us to discover something new—when we allow them to.

This combination stimulates adventurous thinking, and it is central to anyone and any organization that strives to be solutions-oriented. It is also a dynamic way to formulate a progressive narrative that acknowledges the accomplishments of the stakeholders. Such acknowledgments are another one of those small things that quickly add up to no small thing at all.

All normal humans respond to positive feedback. Why else have award ceremonies at the Olympics or wait until after dinner to enjoy a bit of desert? Psychologist Carl Rogers noticed that his patients progressed much faster and farther when he could establish mutual positive regard between himself and them. Providing encouragement is just simple good sense.

Asking, "What else? What is better?" assumes something that is universally apparent, though we regularly ignore it. That is, change is always happening. In asking this question, we take advantage that change is always going on. We assume that tomorrow will be different from today, because honestly, it will be. We can then use change as motivational fuel for our difference engine.

While there are so many things that can contribute to the greater result, noting when others and we are doing things right, multiplies those benefits. The energy generated by a genuine, well-worded compliment (that is, a factual observation and not effusive insincerity), opens the way for all involved to envision and engage even more imaginative and practical solutions, all going forward.

We do mean it when we say words are magic. In essence, so much of human life is based upon words. Even when we are in the midst of activities, we still need to communicate with others what we are doing and what they need to be doing. We are in constant dialogue. Watch a coach on the sidelines of any sports, but especially team sports, and you will see a person in constant communication with their athletes as they run around a court or up and down a field.

Asking, "What else? What is better?" and acknowledging what has been done right keeps us on a positive track and continually refuels our difference engines. When we use all the 5Qs, and especially for difficult problems, we encourage ourselves and others to notice things otherwise overlooked. These may be the very steps that are exactly needed to enhance existing solutions. These 5Qs keep us sensitive to any solution boosting opportunity, no matter how seemingly insignificant it may at first appear.

Two minutes to a difference

Let's now do a 2-minute experiment. To keep it fairly constrained for your first time, try this on a personal level problem. It's better if you don't start out with your biggest granddaddy of a problem, but if you want to tackle one of those, that is okay too.

The first 20 seconds are relatively easy but necessary: You have 20 seconds to get out a pen and paper and prepare a timer, either a stopwatch phone app or a clock with a second-hand sweeper. Alternatively, you can simply estimate the time you use. Each of the eight mini tasks takes about 10 seconds, leaving you with about a minute for the 4th question.

The list of questions below follows the flow of the 5Qs that you have just read. With your pen and paper, make a simple grid with two columns and eight rows (example below). Write 1 – 8 for each row in the first column. Your second and third columns will be larger to accommodate the question and your brief response.

You will only need 10-20 seconds to write your response. Be quick, be terse. The 4th question will take a little longer to do, so you can use about one minute for that. Also, in this exercise, the Miracle Question is modified to keep the experiment brief. We just want you to have a taste of The Matrix the first time using it.

Keep it shorthand, a few words for each response, with a bit more for the Miracle Question when you come to it. Finally, don't worry if your terse responses cannot be understood by anyone else. This exercise is just for you and it is not designed to create comprehensive solutions, but simply to provide you with an introductory experience of it.

There are no wrong answers, just honest and not so honest ones. Try to be as honest as you can and that way your feedback will be clearer in light of the solution you seek. I've included a graph with example answers below that will help you do your own version of this exercise.

The importance of the 5Qs, or the Solutions Matrix™ that we use as a solutions compass, is essentially a muscle-building tool that helps us change our focus and our language, and thus our actions, from problem oriented complaining to solutions focused creating. The former keeps us blaming and shaming others and ourselves while the latter sets in motion thoughts and actions that require positive regard for others and ourselves.

	Question	Answers (< 20 words)
	The Problem *Give your problem or complaint a title*	My boss
1. **Getting Started**	How would you know this approach has been helpful?	I would a better relationship with my boss
2. **The Problem**	What is the problem you have in mind? (1 - 5 words)	My boss treats me unfairly.
3. **Today's baseline**	**Scale / Notice** 0 - 10 where 0 is as bad as the problem could ever be and 10 is the ideal, when the problem no longer happens, where do you feel you are today?	3
4. **Miracle Question**	How you know the miracle happened? **OR** the problem was solved?	My boss would stop threatening to fire me
5. **Exception**	When was a time when you previously solved even parts of the problem or when you experienced exceptions to the problem?	When I made him look good, he gave me credit and stopped threatening me. For a time
6. **Example**	Jot down up to 5 words describing how you did that?	Created successful programs for the hospital system
7. **What Else?**	What else could you do? What is better now?	I decided to find a better boss. I found a new job
8. **Scaling**	On a scale of 0 - 10, where 0 is as bad as could ever be and 10 is the idea, what's the difference you *feel* about your solving this issue?	8

I don't know about you, but when I've chosen the latter, remarkable things have occurred in my life, personally, professionally and socially. From real experience using this Matrix, I am clear as to which I prefer and most consistently use. I hope you have similar experiences using it, and that it makes a valuable difference in your life as well as the important work you do, whether at the UN, out in the corporate world, or in whatever meaningful endeavor in which you are involved.

Appendix B:
Synopsis of John Kotter's
Accelerate Method

John Kotter, Konosuke Matsushita Professor of Leadership, Emeritus, at the Harvard Business School, has focused much of his work on two aspects that one could say lie solidly within the security-driven (L1) side of life. That is, economy (jobs, corporations and the threats to corporate and work life) and urgency (the pace of threats in an increasingly tech-leveraged world that today threatens even—or especially—the largest of traditional companies).

Of course, Kotter has never described his arena of work as addressing the full 3L spectrum of Lizard, Limbic, and Logic or survival-social-strategic parts of the brain. This categorization is my shorthand for noting where on the 3-brain spectrum a particular approach could be said to impact the listener.

His approach, however, did inadvertently touch upon these three aspects of how we function. While addressing our survival needs (urgency), he integrated the social elements of leadership (engaging people by getting buy-in) and then developed a means for strategic process, as in his dual operating system. The latter wisely promotes keen management of existing systems while creating a means to include the extension and expansion of current capacities, scope of impact and influence.

Kotter's work provides an enhanced means for corporate survival appropriate to current global trends. He has laid out this core work in a number of books over a span of years, one of the more recent being *Accelerate* (XLR8). While Kotter's work is one of many in the area of organizational change, I found the simplicity of his approach in line with many of the ideas behind transilient leadership, and importantly, adaptable to the complex environment of the United Nations.

Because the UN is complex, many people suppose that an upgrade or renewal should be equally complex. But this is simply not true and follows from the same kind of false assumption we make about solving problems. In fact, we don't need to know all about a problem to order to solve it. Nor does a complex problem require a complex solution. The best solutions are usually so much simpler than we could ever believe. Isn't that good news?

The following is a synopsis of Kotter's strategy for organizational change. This approach, when spearheaded by transilient leaders, can turn the threats of our times into bold new opportunities that will inspire people worldwide.

We do not need to get bogged down in an in-depth study of his concept. What we do need to know here is that it works well in corporations feeling the heat of their competition and realizing they need to make changes or, quite frankly, find themselves stuck in the tar pits of irrelevance and become extinct like many behemoth dinosaurs have before them.

If this strikes a chord, then delve into Kotter's books or contact Kotter International online.

Summary:
What is Needed for Business Survival

- Whatever is working well now is also being threatened now.
- The pace of threats in a globalizing world coming at business and society-at-large is accelerating.
- Our ability to change also needs to accelerate.
- The old ways of setting and executing new strategies are failing us.
- A solution to this big and serious problem that is already claiming victims such as Borders and Research in Motion (RIM)), is a dual operating system.
- The relevance and future of traditional hierarchical organizations that keep the trains running on time (or, as in the UN, the Member States engaged) are threatened.
- To combat organizational cavitation in the midst of turbulence, these two systems (hierarchy and network)

have to be genuinely dual. Keeping in mind that in reality, the networks are equal in terms of keeping the organization vital, relevant and alive.

• The people who participate in these networks have to be from within the organization, intrinsically motivated and should include at least 5-10% of the entire organization.

Part of Kotter's case for his dual operating system stems from understanding corporate lifecycles.

Building on Corporate Lifecycles: From Networks to Hierarchies

Stage 1 — Networks (no hierarchies)

Stage 2 — Networks, some hierarchies

Stage 3 — Hierarchies, some networks

Stage 4 — All hierarchy no networks

Stage 5 — Adapt or die

Kotter also provides five key principles and Eight Accelerators that drive his Dual Operating System.

The Five Principles Driving
the Dual Operating System

Kotter proposes the formation of a dual operating system of hierarchy and network:

Principle 1 – Many people driving important change do so from everywhere in an organization. They are not just the usual few appointees.

Principle 2 – A "get-to" mindset, not a "have-to" one.

Principle 3 – Action that is head and heart driven, not just head driven.

Principle 4 – Much more leadership, not just more management.

Principle 5 – An inseparable partnership between the hierarchy and the network, not just an enhanced hierarchy.

The Eight Accelerators

Accelerator 1: Urgency Aligned Around A Big Opportunity

Accelerator 2: The Guiding Coalition

Accelerator 3: A Change Vision And Strategic Initiatives

Accelerators 4 & 5: Attracting Volunteers, Driving Initiatives

Accelerators 6–8: Wins, Wins, And More Wins

Find Out More

The Advocacy Algorithm:
Making advocacy and outreach at the UN powerful

The Mindset Module:
Mental Positioning for NGOs working at the UN

The Transilience Masterclass for Change Leaders
Online training, coaching & community

NGO Self Assessment Tool

Solutions Mastery:
Emotional Life Fitness Training

Develop Your Personal Crisis Response Plan:
Personal crisis preparedness training

All available through
www.StrategicSolutions.onl

Glossary

Artificial Intelligence: The science of AI remains more of an endeavor than it is a well-defined area of work. AI's primary goal is to build an intelligence machine. The secondary goal being to better understand the nature of intelligence.[15] With that in mind, the general use of the term includes machine learning and other mechanisms that embody intelligence in machines.

Cyber-Physical Intelligence: This integrates Cyber-Physical Systems and Intelligent Systems. This incorporates intelligent behavior in cyber-physical systems.

Cyber-Physical Systems (CPS): Computing systems interacting with physical processes that are distributed in the real world. These are physical and engineered systems, whose operations are monitored, coordinated, controlled and integrated by a computing and communications core.

ECOSOC: The Economic and Social Council of the United Nations, one of the six original organs of the UN. It consists of fifty-four Members elected by the General Assembly, each serving for a term of three years.

General Assembly: The main organ of the UN consisting of all the Members of the United Nations with each Member having an equal vote.

Intelligent Physical Systems (IPS): IPS are "smart and autonomous systems" cognizant, taskable, reflective, ethical, and knowledge-rich. That is, IPS can be aware of their capabilities and limitations, leading to long-term autonomy requiring minimal or no human operator intervention. For example IPS include, but are not limited to, robotic platforms and networked systems that combine computing, sensing, communication, and actuation.

Intelligent System: An intelligent system is a machine with an embedded, internet-connected computer that has the capacity to gather and analyze data and communicate with other systems.

International Court of Justice: The Court is the principal judicial organ of the United Nations and consists of fifteen members, with no two from the same state.

Meta-Nets: A networked group that innovates around big opportunity initiatives as the organization's response to emergent threats and challenges. The groups are selected volunteers from stakeholders throughout the organization and, where needed, civil society members to provide different perspectives and specific knowledge. They are convened for a specific period of time and their purpose is to articulate and address the big opportunities that new threats and challenges present.

The work of meta-nets is two-fold: First, to develop strategic initiatives in response to new threats the organization is currently unable to address expediently. Secondly, it works to communicate understanding of and develop buy-in for the strategic initiatives they devise.

Secretariat: One of the principal organs of the UN, the Secretary-General being the chief administrative officer of the Organization, appointed by the General Assembly upon the recommendation of the Security Council. The international staff carries out the diverse day-to-day work of the Organization and are not to seek or receive instructions from any government or other authority outside the Organization.

Security Council: One of the six main organs of the UN and consists of fifteen Members of the United Nations with five being permanent (China, Great Britain, France, Russia, USA) and the remaining ten elected by the General Assembly serve for a term of two years. The presidency of the Council rotates monthly, alphabetically.

Solutions Focused Brief Therapy: Solution-focused brief therapy is a clinical therapeutic approach based on solution building rather than problem-solving and is designed to work in no more than six sessions. It explores current resources and future hopes rather than present problems and past causes, and recognizes that each person has all that they need within them to construct solutions.

Solutions Matrix™: A matrix of five questions (5Qs) that act as a compass for the development of solutions focused steps to life's sticky, often emotionally laden problems.

Superintelligence: Regardless of when human-level artificial intelligence arrives, the assumption is that at this point, a superintelligent system that greatly exceeds the cognitive performance of humans in virtually all domains of interest would follow very quickly, possibly even instantaneously. At this point, it would be difficult to control or restrain.[16]

Three Dimensions of Leadership: The three dimensions of leadership include transilience, scope and drivers.

Transilient Leadership: Takes into account all three dimensions of leadership. Transilient leaders also lean into the focus on innovation and change while recognizing the importance of management and maintenance and corresponding systems.

UNODC: United Nations Office of Drugs and Crime. UNODC as an office of the UN Secretariat is mandated to assist Member States in their struggle against illicit drugs, crime and terrorism. UNODC oversees the coordination of the two functional commissions that are policymaking bodies of ECOSOC and UNODC: Commission on Crime Prevention and Criminal Justice and Commission on Narcotic Drugs. It has three pillars of work:

1. Field-based technical cooperation projects to enhance the capacity of Member States to counteract illicit drugs, crime and terrorism

2. Research and analytical work to increase knowledge and understanding of drugs and crime issues and expand the evidence base for policy and operational decisions

3. Normative work to assist States in the ratification and implementation of the relevant international treaties, the development of domestic legislation on drugs, crime and terrorism, and the provision of secretariat and substantive services to the treaty-based and governing bodies.

WSIS: World Summit on the Information Society. Phase One being in Geneva in 2003 and Phase Two as the international conference in Tunis in 2005. WSIS +10 was held in Geneva and efforts are being made to link the WSIS Action Lines with the UN's new Sustainable Development Goals. http://www.itu.int/net4/wsis/sdg/

References

[1] United Nations. 2000. Charter of the United Nations and Statute of the International Court of Justice. New York: United Nations, Office of Public Information. http://search.ebscohost.com/ fifth domain of warfare login.aspx?direct=true&scope=site&db=nleb-k&db=nlabk&AN=348778.

[2] Kotter, John P. 2014. Accelerate: building strategic agility for a faster moving world.

[3] Ibid., p. 20.

[4] Background Note on the "Arria-Formula" Meetings of the Security Council Members, http://www.un.org/en/sc/about/methods/bgarriaformula.shtml

[5] Charter of the United Nations and Statute of the International Court of Justice, Ibid., Article 2.1

[6] Triune brain, https://en.wikipedia.org/wiki/Triune_brain. There are many other resources for discussion of the three brains, but this gives a good place to start.

[7] Lerner, Jennifer S., Ye Li, Piercarlo Valdesolo, and Karim S. Kassam. 2015. "Emotion and Decision Making". Annual Review of Psychology. 66 (1): 799-823.

[8] "Cybersecurity and Development" http://www.un.org/en/development/desa/news/ecosoc/cybersecurity-demands-global-approach.html

[9] "Report of the Group of Governmental Experts on Developments in the Field of Information and Telecommunications in the Context of International Security" A/68/98, June 24, 2013.

[10] "Group of Governmental Experts on Developments in the Field of Information and Telecommunications in the Context of International Security " A/70/174 http://www.un.org/ga/search/view_doc.asp?symbol=A/70/174

[11] Three pillars of UNODC's work program: https://www.unodc.org/unodc/en/about-unodc/index.html?ref=menu2nd

[12] The UN's Global Counter-Terrorism Strategy outlined in a Plan of Action with 4 pillars A/RES/60/288. https://documents-dds-ny.un.org/doc/UNDOC/GEN/N05/504/88/PDF/N0550488.pdf

[13] Jinseop Jang, Jason McSparren & Yuliya Rashchupkina, Global governance: present and future, http://www.palgrave-journals.com/articles/palcomms201545

[14] Kotter, John P., and Lorne A. Whitehead. 2010. Buy-in: saving your good idea from getting shot down. Boston, Mass: Harvard Business Review Press, p 77.

[15] Schank, Roger C. 1987. What Is AI, Anyway? AI Magazine; Vol 8, No 4: Winter 1987; 59. Association for the Advancement of Artificial Intelligence. http://www.aaai.org/ojs/index.php/aimagazine/article/view/623.

[16] Bostrom, Nick. 2014. Superintelligence: paths, dangers, strategies.

About the Author

Dr. Karen Judd Smith is a best-selling author, international speaker, capacity builder, and strategic advisor.

Karen originally hails from Australia but has lived in the United States for more than 30 years. She holds degrees in Physics, History and Philosophy of Science, and Theology. For the practicum part of her doctoral dissertation, she developed the "Advocacy Algorithm," a 36 module online course for international NGOs engaged in advocacy at the UN to shortcut their learning curve in a complex and nuanced environment.

Karen has spent her adult life developing and overseeing international projects, often associated with international peace and justice issues with relevant to the UN and its global agenda. She is the author of "Change !t Up," and "Making Your NGO's Advocacy Powerful" and now, "United Nations Unlocked: The Missing Link the UN Needs to Tackle Global Terrorism and the Coming Tech Tsunami."

To supplement her work, she has, over the years, also developed a number of online courses for building personal and team capacities for dealing with crisis and change. These provide foundational materials for capacity building training and projects and are available through the www.NGO-Academy.org, an online training site for social entrepreneurs she began in 2010.

Over the years, Karen has spoken extensively in more than 20 countries promoting strategic and innovative social initiatives and currently consults for international NGOs and entrepreneurs who take their role as global citizens seriously and wish to leverage their resources optimally.

She currently serves as the NY Chair of the Alliance of NGOs of Crime Prevention and Criminal Justice, is the lead for the Alliance's Counter Terrorism and Cyberwar and continues to push for greater engagement between the tech community and projects designed to defuse violent extremism and the global security arena.

In the midst of all this seriousness, Karen balances her life with gardening, feeding the hummingbirds and wild turkeys, fending off VR invaders with her grown sons, learning about the latest in biotech research from her daughter and competing with her husband in tennis and Mario Kart. Between colleagues, friends, and family, she enjoys a wide variety of political and tech banter, online, around the world and in person over a cuppa. One item on her bucket list is to make her 20th skydive a full family affair.

For more on this book and transilient leadership, please visit www.StrategicSolutions.onl.